THE EXCLUDED BOOKS OF THE BIBLE

- UPDATED -

WHY WERE THESE SACRED TEXTS HIDDEN FROM THE WORLD FOR CENTURIES?

SEAN CASTEEL

THE EXCLUDED
BOOKS OF
THE BIBLE
UPDATED

Sean Casteel

INNER LIGHT/GLOBAL COMMUNICATIONS

THE EXCLUDED BOOKS OF THE BIBLE
- UPDATED -
BY SEAN CASTEEL

Please address any questions about this book to:
mrufo8@hotmail.com

Timothy Green Beckley: Editorial Director

Carol Ann Rodriguez: Publishers Assistant

Tim R. Swartz - Interior Formatting and Cover Design

Visit Mr. UFOs Secret Files on You Tube
https://www.youtube.com/user/MRUFO1100

For Free Subscription to The Conspiracy Journal Write:

Tim Beckley/Global Communications

Box 753, New Brunswick, NJ 08903

Email: mrufo8@hotmail.com

www.ConspiracyJournal.Com

CONTENTS

Who Excluded The Excluded Books Of The Bible?
By Sean Casteel

You are about to embark on a journey through some holy texts that you may likely have never heard of, let alone actually read. They bear a great deal of resemblance to more familiar books of the Old and New Testaments in that they take up the subject of Yahweh and his relationship with the Jews, but they also provide alternate versions of the story of Jesus Christ and the true nature of his teachings.

While many at the time considered the books discussed herein to be sacred, they were nevertheless excluded from the Biblical canon that we know today. The process of finalizing the canon was a lengthy one and occurred over many centuries. For our purposes here, I choose as a starting point the story of the Roman Emperor Constantine.

CONSTANTINE'S CONVERSION

Constantine reigned over Rome from 306 to 337 A.D. Prior to his ascension to the throne, Christianity was an outlaw religion and calling oneself a Christian was literally a crime. The first recorded official persecution of Christianity happened in A.D. 64, when Emperor Nero attempted to falsely blame Christians for the Great Fire of Rome. Thereafter, Christians suffered sporadic and localized persecutions for two and a half centuries. Their refusal to participate in various established forms of Roman cult worship was considered treason and thus punishable by execution.

In the year 312 A.D., Constantine was leading his troops into the Battle of Milvian Bridge, which provided an important route over the Tiber River in what is now Italy. Constantine was pitted against a rival Emperor, Maxentius, in a war for the control of Rome. Just before the fighting commenced, Constantine looked up at the sun and saw a cross of light above it and the words, "In this sign, you will conquer." Constantine commanded his troops to add a Christian symbol called a "Chi-Rho" to their shields, after which his soldiers were victorious.

Constantine interpreted his victory as a sign of favor from the Christian God and, upon his return to the Roman capitol, he did not carry out the traditional pagan sacrifices and rituals intended to celebrate a general's victorious return to Rome. In 313, Constantine declared with the Edict of Milan that "it was proper that the Christians and all others have liberty to follow that mode of religion which to each of them appeared best."

Now that being Christian was no longer a crime, Constantine became a patron of the early church, providing financial support and permitting the building of numerous houses of worship and basilicas. He lightened the tax burdens of Christian clergy and promoted many Christians to high office.

THE FIRST COUNCIL OF NICEA

But Constantine's embracing of Christianity was not without problems. There was much bickering and dissension regarding what fundamental Christian belief should consist of. In 325 A.D., in an attempt to unify the warring factions, Constantine convened the First Council of Nicea, attended by hundreds of bishops, priests and other clergy. One of their essential points of disagreement concerned which gospel was to be accepted, the Gospel of John or the Gospel of Thomas?

According to an online review of Elaine Pagels' *"Beyond Belief,"* by book critic Mary W. Matthews, a church official named Bishop Irenaeus heavily promoted John as the true gospel and denounced the Gospel of Thomas as "evil" because its approach was too egalitarian. John allows Christian doctrine to be kept firmly under the control of the church by promoting the establishment of a hierarchy: God, Jesus, priest, deacon, ordinary folks.

"In other words," Matthews writes, "Irenaeus' great achievement was the development of what we now call the canon – this is holy scripture; this isn't – and the 'stabilization' of Christianity. Quality control. The First Council of Nicea is memorable for having settled the first great controversy of Christianity: Was Jesus God, part of the Holy Trinity, or was he merely LIKE God? The Nicene Creed tells us that John won: Jesus is not merely like God, he is 'of one substance' with God."

As part of the Nicene Creed, this position had the official stamp of approval of both the Church Establishment and Emperor Constantine, who had set himself up as the unofficial but nevertheless openly recognized head of the church.

"There was no salvation outside the church," Matthews writes. "The church alone knew the truth. The truth was found in John's portrayal of Jesus as the only route to God, not in Thomas' more egalitarian teachings."

EMBRACING THE REJECTED BOOKS IN GOOD FAITH

This book, however, deals with writings like the abovementioned Gospel of Thomas and many others that "never made the cut" with the Council of Nicea or the other similar convocations that came later. Why is the Gospel of Thomas "evil," for example? Why not read these books with the same reverence accorded to the official Biblical canon? What's so wrong with an approach to Christ that views his followers as equals and doesn't place true believers in the grip of an authoritarian priestly hierarchy? Why should we deny women their rightful, equal place among the male followers of Jesus? Why is the concept of Jesus as a mere mortal, subject to the same human frailties as the rest of us, somehow damnably sacrilegious?

This more open, inquisitive approach to what is truly sacred is well-stated by Elaine Pagels, who won the National Book Award for her groundbreaking book "*The Gnostic Gospels*": "What I have come to love in the wealth and diversity of our religious traditions – and the communities that sustain them – is that they offer the testimony of innumerable people to spiritual discovery, encouraging us, in Jesus' words, to 'seek and you shall find.'"

What follows in "*The Excluded Books of the Bible*" is an analysis of certain selected Gnostic Christian works as well as a look at a trio of books left out of the Old Testament. It begins with the story of how a cache of long lost Gnostic texts was discovered in Egypt in 1945, which is followed by a brief overview of what "Gnosis" is all about, before diving into chapters devoted to the "outlaw" versions of Jesus and his message for humanity.

If you're seeking new ways to relate to God and his only begotten Son, these "forbidden" scriptures are a good place to start.

Chapter One
Unearthing A Mystery

- Learn the history of the discovery of a cache of manuscripts in Egypt that has changed forever the way we perceive the life of Jesus Christ.

- Does knowledge of ourselves lead directly to knowledge of God? Read what the secrets of "Gnosis" reveal to those who search deeply in its mysteries.

- Was the Church as we know it today established for the sake of political control and not for the salvation of the individual?

What determines whether a book is canonized scripture or just the ravings of a heretic? Who makes that decision for the many believers looking for a reasonable approach to questions of salvation and righteous behavior? Should we trust our individual instincts regarding our worship of God or follow the leadership of an organized clergy? What is the ultimate truth behind the many divergent accounts of the life of Jesus Christ?

This book will grapple with those and other issues by examining an often overlooked school of religious thought—the Gnostics of early Christianity, a movement that was steadfastly denounced and vilified by the established church and whose writings were buried away in Egypt for nearly 1600 years. The discovery of those hidden texts has changed not only the way we think about that historical moment in time, but has also given us a new perspective on the sayings and deeds of Jesus that was impossible before.

THE DISCOVERY AT NAG HAMMADI

The story of how the Gnostic scriptures were found is almost as fascinating as the books themselves.

James M. Robinson, writing in the introduction to the English translation of the complete cache of manuscripts, tells the tale this way:

It was December of 1945, a time when the peasants of the Nag Hammadi region of Upper Egypt fertilize their crops. Two such farmers, the brothers Muhammad and Khalifah, were digging for a kind of soft soil that is used there as a fertilizer when they came upon the jar, made of red earthenware and about a meter high, containing the books. The jar had been hidden beneath a fallen boulder for more than a millennium. Muhammad was at first hesitant to break the jar, fearing that it may have housed a demon. But after thinking that the jar could possibly have contained gold, he decided to take his chances and smashed the jar open.

"Out swirled golden-like particles that disappeared into the sky," Robinson wrote. "Neither jinns nor gold but perhaps papyrus fragments!"

Muhammad wrapped the books in his cloak and took them home. Then the story rewinds to a time six months before, May 7, 1945, to be exact. That's when the father of the two brothers killed a marauder as he stood watch over irrigation equipment in the fields. The father was killed himself the next day in blood vengeance.

"About a month after the discovery of the books," Robinson continued, "a peasant named Ahmad fell asleep sitting in the heat of the day on the side of the road near Muhammad's house, a jar of sugar-cane molasses for sale beside him. A neighbor pointed him out to Muhammad as the murderer of his father. He ran home and alerted his brothers and widowed mother, who had told her seven sons to keep their mattocks sharp. The family fell upon their victim, hacked off his limbs bit by bit, ripped out his heart, and devoured it among them, as the ultimate act of blood revenge."

Ahmad, the brothers' victim, was the son of the local sheriff, and Muhammad feared having his house searched and the books discovered, so he passed some of them along to a local priest for safekeeping. The books would eventually be purchased by a series of Egyptian antiquities dealers, but not until after Muhammad's mother had burned a portion of them, thinking either that they were worthless or a possible source of bad luck. It wasn't until 1970 that a committee was formed to supervise the translation of the books from their original language of Coptic, which is the name given to Greek after it has been translated into Egyptian.

Now that the job of translating the books has been completed, a new era of studying their contents has just begun. We await the verdict of scholars in our own time as well as that of the scholars to come.

But whether we ever actually solve the many mysteries the Nag Hammadi find poses to us, we can at least rest assured in the knowledge that some of the world's greatest scholars of ancient writings are doing their utmost to decipher the truth.

WHAT DOES "GNOSIS" MEAN?

Gnosis is simply the Greek word for "knowledge." In the same way that those who claim to know nothing about the nature of God and reality in general are called "agnostics," literally "not knowing," the person who claims to know such things is called "Gnostic," according to Elaine Pagels in her landmark book *The Gnostic Gospels*.

"But gnosis is not primarily rational knowledge," Pagels cautions. "The Greek language distinguishes between scientific or reflective knowledge ('He knows mathematics') and knowing through observation or experience ('He knows me'), which is gnosis. As the Gnostics use the term, we could translate it as 'insight,' for gnosis involves an intuitive process of knowing oneself. And to know oneself, they claimed, is to know human nature and human destiny."

Pagels takes that basic formula one step further.

"Yet to know oneself," she writes, "at the deepest level, is simultaneously to know God; this is the secret of gnosis."

Pagels then quotes the Gnostic teacher Monoiumus, who declares: "Abandon the search for God and the creation and other matters of a similar sort. Look for him by taking yourself as the starting point. Learn who it is within you who makes everything his own and says, 'My God, my mind, my thought, my soul, my body.' Learn the source of sorrow, joy, love, hate. If you carefully investigate these matters, you will find them in yourself."

That inner-directed viewpoint seems fairly tame in our time, but among the ancient Christians those sentiments were considered blasphemy and heresy, and the Gnostics feared persecution from many elements that they had considered to be their fellow Christians. There existed a huge theological divide over the issue of the value of the experience of the individual looking inwardly to find God as opposed to finding God in the collective experience of the catholic or universal church.

As is nearly always the case, history is written by the winners, and until the discovery of the Gnostic books in Nag Hammadi, the only historical accounts available about the Gnostic movement were to be found in the writings of the various orthodox religious leaders and historians who denounced them.

WHY WERE THE GNOSTICS SO DIFFERENT?

In addition to their focus on the subjective nature of genuine religious experience, the Gnostics also held to other beliefs that were hated by the orthodox. The Gnostics deified the feminine element of God, for instance, believing in God as both the Father *and* the Mother. They believed that Creation, the physical world, was created by an evil god, the equivalent of Satan, and that suffering, labor and death were not the fault of mankind's sin but of the wicked designer of reality. Some Gnostics did not believe in a literal resurrection, choosing instead to see Christ's rising from the dead in symbolic terms.

Pagels points out that the orthodox church also held to what would seem to be some strange doctrines, such as the belief that God is perfectly good and yet created a world that includes pain, injustice and death; that Jesus was born of a virgin mother; that after being executed by Pontius Pilate, he rose from the grave on the third day.

But the source of the conflict between the Gnostics and the orthodoxy, according to Pagels, was not just the many differences of opinion regarding religious and philosophical issues about Jesus. It was about control, specifically political control. A Christianity that required faith in a central church was much more likely to exert control over its masses of believers than one that counseled each individual to look within himself for answers.

Which again is why the discovery of the Gnostic scriptures is so crucial, because it offers an alternative view of Christ, a view long hidden beneath the sands of Egypt, suppressed by the religious authorities of its time, and excluded from the Bible as we know it today. This book will attempt to give an overview of the Gnostics, their beliefs, and their relevance to today's world, and to break through the censorship that has existed since ancient times.

Chapter Two
The Gospel of Thomas: On More Familiar Ground

- Did Jesus come to cast fire on the world? Is social and political unrest a sign of his hand in world events?
- Just who did the disciples of Jesus perceive him to be? An angel? A wise philosopher?
- Why was the Apostle Thomas instructed to keep what Jesus had told him in private a secret from the other disciples?

For those unfamiliar with extra-Biblical texts, it may be helpful to start with the Gnostic book The Gospel of Thomas, since it plainly echoes and repeats many of the sayings of Jesus that appear in the canonical gospels. The Gospel of Thomas is hard to place in any one historical context. It seems at times to predate the New Testament versions, perhaps drawing on the same original sources, but at other moments it is said to have been influenced by at least a barebones knowledge of what the New Testament reported as the words of the living Christ.

Despite its similarity to the canonized versions, it was apparently deemed heretical by the Orthodox Church leadership that came later, perhaps because it offers no narrative or storyline, but simply catalogs the sayings of Jesus as he is heard speaking to his disciples.

Jesus addresses the subject of the Kingdom of Heaven throughout The Gospel of Thomas, mainly in parable, but says quite early on that the kingdom is within the individual and is already spread out upon the earth, though no one can see it. Which again is found in similar terms in the New Testament.

THE WORLD ON FIRE

Another point of repetition concerns Christ's warnings about the apocalypse.

In verses 10 and 11, he says, "I have cast fire upon the world, and see, I am guarding it until it blazes. This heaven will pass away, and the one above it will pass away. The dead are not alive, and the living will not die. In the days when you consumed what is dead, you made it what is alive. When you come to dwell in the light, what will you do?"

One is reminded of the often-reported vision shown to alien abductees of a world set on fire, a warning of the End Times in what is perhaps intended to be a simple visual expression of the idea of apocalypse. Perhaps Jesus is conveying that same primal image of doom with just a few well-chosen words?

Verse 16 makes a similar declaration: "Men think, perhaps, that it is peace which I have come to cast upon the world. They do not know that it is dissension which I have come to cast upon the earth: fire, sword, and war. For there will be five in a house; three will be against two, and two against three, the father against the son and the son against the father. And they shall stand solitary."

The kind of social divisiveness Jesus seems to be talking about is something fearsome indeed. It smacks of a kind of Orwellian, *1984* existence in which even close family members are made to betray one another to a police state government where individual rights are as nothing and loyalty to a Big Brother-type beast is required from all. The informant that does you in could easily be your father or your son, two of a household in conflict with the three others in a deadly game of loyalty to state versus loyalty to family and friends.

One shudders to think of such a form of oppression, an emotional and psychological concentration camp where all the natural impulses of love are put on ice and grow cold. Did Jesus somehow see into the 21st Century and its withering of familial love?

JESUS IS EVERYWHERE

But there is more than just a dark prophetic picture in The Gospel of Thomas. In verse 77, Jesus says that he is everywhere and is everything.

"It is I who am the light which is above them all. It is I who am the all. From me did the all come forth, and unto me did the all extend. Split a piece of wood, and I am there. Lift up the stone, and you will find me there."

One can see that Jesus is making a declaration similar to his saying "I am the Light of the World" in the New Testament, though the references to wood and stone do not appear there. Still, it's a refreshing variation and quite nicely poetic.

Earlier in The Gospel of Thomas (verse 13) there occurs a scene in which Jesus asks his disciples to "compare me to someone and tell me who I am like."

"Simon Peter said to him, 'You are like a righteous angel.'

"Matthew said to him, 'You are like a wise philosopher.'

"Thomas said to him, 'Master, my mouth is wholly incapable of saying whom you are like.'

"Jesus said, 'I am not your master. Because you have drunk, you have become intoxicated from the bubbling spring which I have measured out.' And he took him and withdrew, and told him three things. When Thomas returned to his companions, they asked him, 'What did Jesus say to you?' Thomas said to them, 'If I tell you one of the things which he told me, you will pick up stones and throw them at me; a fire will come out of the stones and burn you up.'"

The meaning of this one is a little elusive to say the least, but the image of stones issuing an avenging fire is extremely powerful. It seems to imply that the truths Jesus would say in private to just one disciple would produce a violent rage in the others. One wonders whether the reality Jesus keeps hidden would produce the same anger and disbelief in us. Could we, as they saying goes, handle the truth?

Chapter Three
The Woman of Thunder

- What is the true nature of the feminine principle? Is woman found simultaneously in extremes of good and evil?

- Will a future race somehow embody the strange opposites expressed in the Gnostic book The Thunder, Perfect Mind? Is mankind to be transformed together and collectively?

- Just as there is a God the Father, should we be open to the idea of God the Mother?

Though it was discovered along with the Gnostic scriptures in the find at Nag Hammadi, the book The Thunder, Perfect Mind is hard for scholars to classify. They note, for example, that there are few to none overt references that can be called either Judaic or Christian, and theorize that the book may come from a Gnostic school of thought that either predates the later Biblical tradition or somehow exists outside of it. But there is no denying its impact, its profundity, or its relevance to our present day.

THE VIRGIN WHORE

The Thunder, Perfect Mind is the first-person statements of some sort of female entity who speaks in beautifully organized opposites, what are sometimes called "dichotomies." The style is a familiar one often found in ancient writings, but the frankness with which it addresses the female condition has no peer in the canonized scripture.

"I was sent forth from the power," the book begins, "and I have come to those who reflect upon me, and I have been found among those who seek after me . . . . Be on your guard! Do not be ignorant of me. For I am the first and the last, I am the honored one and the scorned one. I am the whore and the holy one. I am the wife and the virgin. I am the mother and the daughter. I am the members of my mother. I am the barren one and many are her sons. I am she whose wedding is great, and I have not taken a husband. I am the midwife and she who does not bear. I am the solace of my labor pains."

The conflict between the various pairs of opposites, as in "I am the whore and the holy one," cuts to core of the inner battle in the female psyche, obviously, but it also liberates with its acceptance of the inevitable and ongoing struggle. Again, there is no precise name given to the woman whose voice speaks in The Thunder, Perfect Mind, but it has been suggested that perhaps we should hear in the book the voice of Eve speaking, declaring from the primordial mists what it means to be a woman cast out of paradise.

Another theory posits that perhaps we are dealing with Sophia, the Greek personification of wisdom, who is eternally the female of the species.

In either case, one can see that this is something the Orthodox Church would not hesitate to exclude from the canon. The paternalistic, even misogynistic attitude of the early church fathers surely could not have easily accepted a female declaration of independence and even spiritual domination as expressed in The Thunder, Perfect Mind. This is a far cry from Mary, the mother of God, whose purity and status above the average woman were undisputed by the Orthodox Church.

AN END TIMES WARNING?

"For I am knowledge and ignorance, I am shame and boldness, I am shameless and I am ashamed, I am strength and I am fear, I am war and peace. Give heed to me. I am the one who is disgraced and the great one. Give heed to my poverty and my wealth. Do not be arrogant to me when I am cast upon the earth, and you will find me in those that are to come. And do not look upon me on the dung-heap, nor go and leave me cast out, and you will find me in the kingdoms . . . . but I, I am compassionate and I am cruel."

Again the dichotomies are beautifully juxtaposed against one another, but this section also seems to include a bit of prophecy. "You will find me in those that are to come," the woman says. Is this a warning about the future of mankind? Will we somehow be physically transformed? One is reminded that the alien genetics program seems geared to producing an alien/human hybrid creature intended to be an improvement over the standard homo sapiens of today, especially in spiritual terms. Or as the Apostle Paul says, "We shall all be changed." Whether from the extraterrestrial or the Biblical perspective, some basic change in the makeup of man seems inevitable, and perhaps the mysterious woman of The Thunder, Perfect Mind is characterized as female precisely because of her role as the mother who will bear the new mankind.

"I am the one who has been hated everywhere, and who has been loved everywhere. I am the one who they call Life, and you have called Death. I am the one whom they call the Law, and you have called Lawlessness. I am the one whom you have pursued, and I am the one whom you have seized. I am the one whom you have scattered, and you have gathered me together."

Here we are charged with the errors of our ways. We have failed to perceive that the woman is life and a life-giving law. We have pursued her as though she were a fugitive, and have scattered her to the winds even as we have gathered her together.

DUALITY AND BEYOND

It should be pointed out that this kind of apparently self-contradictory word game is perhaps the purest approach to truth. Things are both black and white at the same time. We continually contradict ourselves and move from one extreme to the other as though we simply don't have the sheer force of will to be simply one thing or the other.

The late great scholar of myth Joseph Campbell quite astutely argued that this view of things imposes a bewildering state of mind that he called "duality." Campbell said further that it is in transcendence above duality that we find the most complete forms of spiritual truth. For instance, when Christ declares in the Sermon on the Mount, "The rain falls on the just and the unjust." The rain symbolizes an absolute truth that stands above and separate from "the just and the unjust."

We look for that same kind of unifying truth in The Thunder, Perfect Mind and see it most closely represented in the closing sections.

"Hear me, you hearers, and learn of my words, you who know me. I am the hearing that is attainable to everything; I am the speech that cannot be grasped. I am the name of the sound and the sound of the name. I am the sign of the letter and the designation of the division . . . . Give heed then, you hearers, and you also, the angels, and those who have been sent, and you spirits who have arisen from the dead. For I am the one who alone exists, and I have no one who will judge me. For many are the pleasant forms which exist in numerous sins, and incontinencies, and disgraceful passions, and fleeting pleasures, which men embrace until they become sober and go up to their resting place. And they will find me there, and they will live, and they will not die again."

Here we hear the mysterious female declare herself to have powers similar to what the Old Testament testifies of God the Father. Are we dealing with some form of God the Mother? Is this a female entity somehow equal in power to the more familiar Yahweh thundering down from the mountaintop? The theme of feminine spirituality and its power and place in the scheme of things will be discussed elsewhere in this book, and we shall try to ignore the sound of the church fathers groaning in dismay.

Chapter Four
Mary, Beloved of Jesus

- Was Mary Magdalene Jesus' favorite of his disciples? Did Jesus tell her secrets for her ears only?
- What kind of dissension did Mary Magdalene stir up among the other apostles? Was Saint Peter merely jealous of her?
- Why would it be logical to assume that Jesus may have loved Mary Magdalene in romantic terms? Was he so different from the other men of his time?

The role of women in the Excluded Books of the Bible is enormously complex, and is acted out on many levels. The issue of whether Jesus might have in fact preferred his female disciple, Mary Magdalene, over the others is one of the main questions discussed in the Gospel of Mary, another unique book found in the Gnostic trove at Nag Hammadi.

Unfortunately, only a few pages of the complete text of The Gospel of Mary still exist today, but enough remains that a narrative structure can still be discerned from what has survived. First, Jesus appears to his disciples shortly after his resurrection and instructs them to go out and preach the gospel. The disciples immediately become discouraged, asking if the earthly powers-that-be would not spare Jesus for the message he gave, how could they hope to escape death themselves?

At this point, Mary speaks up and tries to offer encouragement. Peter then asks Mary if Jesus had taught her anything in private which he had not taught the men. Mary begins to recite a vision she has had recently, a vision that is essentially a dialogue with Christ.

She goes before a tough audience, one not often disposed to taking the words of a woman with the same weight of truth as with a man.

But Mary soldiers on bravely nonetheless.

WHAT JESUS REVEALS TO MARY

Christ tells her that visions are not seen by the soul or the spirit, but by the mind, which is between the two. After this saying by Jesus, several pages are missing. But there quickly follows a fragmentary tale of "the soul" rising above four powers who are said to stand in the way of the soul's attempts to reach transcendence. The fourth and final power has seven elements, which are first, darkness, the second, desire, the third, ignorance, the fourth, the excitement of death, the fifth, the kingdom of the flesh, the sixth, the foolish wisdom of the flesh, and the seventh, wrathful wisdom.

"These are the seven powers of wrath," Mary continues. "They ask the soul, 'Whence do you come, slayer of men, or where are you going, conqueror of space?' The soul answered and said, 'What binds me has been slain, and what surrounds me has been overcome, and my desire has been ended, and ignorance has died. In a world, I was released from a world, and in a type from a heavenly type, and from the fetter of oblivion, which is transient. From this time on I will attain to the rest of the time, of the season, of the eon, in silence.'"

THE UNBELIEF OF THE OTHERS

After reciting her vision, Mary falls silent, having accomplished the purpose Jesus had when he spoke to her. The disciple Andrew immediately speaks up and denies the truth of what Mary has said, and calls her teachings "strange." Peter then asks if it is possible that Jesus spoke to a woman without the knowledge of the other disciples.

"Did he prefer her to us?" Peter asks.

At which point Mary begins to weep, and asks Peter if he really thinks she is a liar.

Then Levi speaks up for Mary, admonishing Peter and saying that Peter had always been "hot tempered."

"Now I see you contending against the woman," Levi says, "like the adversaries. But if the Savior made her worthy, who are you indeed to reject her? Surely the Savior knows her very well. That is why he loved her more than us. Rather let us be ashamed and put on the perfect man, and acquire him for ourselves as he commanded us, and preach the gospel, not laying down any other rule or other law beyond what the Savior said."

The Gospel of Mary then ends with a brief sentence saying they began to go forth and preach as had been commanded them.

There is no complete resolution of the conflict between male and female here, no ultimate decision as to whether or not woman are to be considered the inferiors of men. But there is at least the opening of a lively debate that argues for the possibility of equality for women. The obvious preference of the author of the Gospel of Mary is that Mary's testimony be given the authority of a sound teaching, with Andrew and Peter arguing for the outmoded conservative anti-female doctrines of the past.

JESUS SAYS IT WITH A KISS

There is a similar scene recounted in The Gospel of Philip, in which the disciples confront Jesus about his preference for Mary.

"The companion of the Savior is Mary Magdalene. But Christ loved her more than all the disciples, and used to kiss her often on the mouth. The rest of the disciples were offended. They said to him, 'Why do you love her more than all of us?' The Savior answered and said to them, 'Why do I not love you as I love her? When a blind man and one who sees are both together in darkness, they are no different from one another. When the light comes, then he who sees will see the light, and he who is blind will remain in darkness.'"

The disciples are apparently supposed to wait until the light of Jesus and his preference for Mary is shown to them. Patience is called for, and a longing to see beyond any blindness one may be suffering from. In other words, this mystery will slowly reveal itself in its own time to those prepared to receive it.

WHAT ARE WE TO BELIEVE ABOUT JESUS AND MARY?

But perhaps that mystery is not quite so dark after all. Many Biblical scholars have concluded that Jesus would have been more of a typical Jewish man of his time than he is given credit for. As a Jew of thirty years of age, he would be expected, even duty-bound, to take a wife and ply a trade. It is said in the New Testament that Jesus and his followers lived by charity, perhaps even taking sustenance from the various Roman welfare programs of the time, and there is no evidence that he ever worked for a living beyond his career as preacher and healer. Whether or not Jesus ever took a wife, his attraction to Mary and even the moments of public physical affection for her described above would not be out of the question.

When it is said that Jesus would often kiss Mary on the mouth, this again is different from the customary kiss of greeting that was part of the manners and mores of ancient Judea. The socially appropriate kiss was a quick peck on the forehead, so

Jesus' overtly sexual kiss on Mary's mouth implies much more than a social obligation.

Much recent Biblical scholarship has blazed a similar trail, trying, among other things, to exonerate Mary Magdalene from the false accusation that she was a prostitute prior to meeting Jesus and joining his group of followers. She is perhaps deserving of even more veneration than she has yet received, since there does exist evidence, although banned from the Bible, that Jesus singled her out as his favorite because she was literally worthy of being so chosen. The complete absorption of this tantalizing possibility would force us to rewrite much of the way reality is currently viewed, whether among the secular or the sacred, and give women a position altogether new among their male counterparts.

Chapter Five
A Fragment Of The Time To Come

- Did Jesus have foreknowledge of a future generation, one that would be beset by wars and political turmoil?
- Are we to await the coming of a new breed of children, prophesied in both the Gnostic scriptures and by the prophet Nostradamus?
- Do alien breeding experiments have a role to play in the fulfillment of prophecies of a future race?

There are many references in the Excluded Books of the Bible to future events, to an apocalyptic time of warfare, destruction and the fulfillment of Jesus' promise to take peace from the earth and stir up many conflicts on the way to the coming of the Kingdom of Heaven. In the Gnostic book called The Apocryphon of James, Jesus makes another interesting promise about the future world.

The Apocryphon of James, which is said to be authored by the brother of Jesus familiar from the New Testament stories, consists mainly of Jesus' words to his disciples delivered more than 500 days after his resurrection. A lot of what Jesus has to say here is confusing and self-contradictory, and when the disciples ask for clarification, Jesus tells them to disdain his negative remarks and take the more positive comments to heart joyfully.

Toward the end of this strange little book, Jesus begins to make a farewell speech.

"I shall ascend to the place from whence I came. But you, when I was eager to go, have cast me out, and instead of accompanying me, you have pursued me. But pay heed to the glory that awaits me, and having opened your heart, listen to the hymns that await me up in the heavens, for today I must take my place at the right hand of the Father. But I have said my last word to you, and I shall depart from you, for a chariot of spirit has borne me aloft."

We can perhaps read in Jesus' words "a chariot of spirit" something similar to Elijah's "chariot of fire," and make the usual connections to a modern-day UFO as the system of transportation Jesus refers to.

THE COMING OF A FUTURE RACE

"And from this moment on," Jesus continues, "I shall strip myself that I may clothe myself. But give heed: blessed are they who have proclaimed the Son before his descent, that, when I have come, I might ascend again. Thrice blessed are they who were proclaimed by the Son before they came to be, that you might have a portion among them."

We should pay careful attention here to Jesus as he says, "those who were proclaimed by the Son *before they came to be*," as it is a reference to a future generation who Jesus is "proclaiming," or announcing triumphantly.

"Having said these words, he departed. But we bent our knees, I and Peter, and gave thanks and sent our hearts upwards to heaven. We heard with our ears, and saw with our eyes, the noise of wars and a trumpet blare and a great turmoil."

Again, a simple statement of End Times warfare and apocalyptic conflict.

"And when we had passed beyond that place, we sent our minds farther upwards, and saw with our eyes and heard with our ears hymns and angelic benedictions and angelic rejoicing. And heavenly majesties were singing praise, and we too rejoiced. After this, again, we wished to send our spirit upward to the Majesty, and after ascending we were not permitted to see or hear anything, for the other disciples called us and asked us, 'What did you hear from the Master? And what has he said to you? And where did he go?'"

The answer James and Peter give to the disciples who had stayed behind is a beautiful mystery.

"But we answered them, 'He has ascended and has given us a pledge and promised life to us all and revealed to us children who are to come after us, after bidding us love them, as we would be saved for their sakes.' And when they heard this, they indeed believed the revelation, but were displeased about those to be born. And so, not wishing to give them offense, I sent each one to another place. But I myself went up to Jerusalem, praying that I might obtain a portion among the beloved who will be made manifest."

THE END TIMES/NOSTRADAMUS CONNECTION

These children of the future that Jesus tells James and Peter about are echoed by a passage from *The Untold Story—Nostradamus' Unpublished Prophecies* (Inner Light Books, 1983.) The book claims to be prophecies that the famed seer left out of the main body of his work because they were too shocking to reveal, even in the enigmatic language of his Centuries. While it is probably impossible to completely authenticate this previously unpublished manuscript, it may be helpful to draw the reader's attention to this fragment of the future according to Nostradamus: "A new breed descends in gratitude. Conflagration in the heavens . . ."

Could this "new breed" Nostradamus describes be the same "children who will come after us," as they are called here in The Apocryphon of James? What about the hostile reaction of some of the disciples to the news as delivered by Jesus? Is this perhaps a natural reaction to the sheer strangeness of these future children? Would we feel any differently were we to actually see these children of the future?

Ever since Budd Hopkins released his landmark work on alien abduction, **Intruders**, in 1987, UFO researchers have time and again run across what appears to be a deliberate program to breed human/alien hybrid children and to assimilate them among us at some indeterminate point in the future. Could these half human, half alien children be the fulfillment of Jesus' prophecy to James and Peter? Are they so strange in appearance that one's natural tendency is to shun them? And are these future children yet so spiritually advanced that we as everyday, run-of-the-mill homos sapiens cannot hope to compete with their advanced state of being? Remember that Jesus instructed the two disciples to "love" these future children, as we will be saved for their sakes. James says he travels to Jerusalem to pray that he be a part of this promised generation when it is made manifest. It seems the future belongs to them and we are lucky to be able to go along for the ride.

The Apocryphon of James raises many questions we cannot answer at this point, admittedly. And it is equally obvious that this is the kind of scripture that the Orthodox Church later rejected without hesitation and banned from the Bible without looking back. Perhaps we are living in an age from which we can see a little better into the mysteries this excluded book presents us with, and we should hold out some degree of hope for these future children Jesus prophesies to us about. Even though it made them resentful, even the nay-saying disciples still believed the message was the truth, after all, and it may be the kind of truth from which there is—blissfully—no escape.

Chapter Six
The Coming Of The Illuminator

- What did Adam himself have to say about his fall from grace? How did he and Eve react to their new state of punishment?
- Is God the Creator at fault for the evil and injustice of this world? Should we seek a higher power then the one that made us?
- Who is the Illuminator, and where does he come from? Why does he do battle with the Maker Of All That Is?

The Apocalypse of Adam is one of those few books found at Nag Hammadi that may deal with a savior figure other than Christ. Scholars date it as being written quite early in comparison to the other books, and while it has obvious Jewish influences, especially evident in its retelling of some of the stories from Genesis, there are no clear-cut references to the historical Jesus or to other Christian doctrines.

The book is structured as a "last testament" in which Adam, near death, begins by telling his son Seth of the fall from grace and the expulsion of Adam and Eve from the Garden of Eden.

"And the glory in our hearts left us," Adam says to Seth, "me and your mother Eve, along with the first knowledge that breathed within us . . . . Since that time, we learned about dead things, like men. Then we recognized the god who had created us. For we were not strangers to his powers. And we served him in fear and slavery. And after these events, we became darkened in our hearts."

Adam, though he speaks in harsh terms of serving God "in fear and slavery," is nonetheless telling it as it is. This serves as an extremely honest insight into what anyone would have felt like having undergone the experience of being cast out from paradise by an angry God.

Adam does not speak in loving terms of a loving God, and one again realizes that in spite of how strange it is to see such a negative portrayal of God in Eden, it is nevertheless very realistic in the human terms of Adam.

DELIVERANCE FROM GOD?

Adam next says he is visited by three angels, who prophesy to him about the coming great flood and Noah's role in saving mankind. From the seed of Noah and his sons will come the Illuminator.

"Once again, the Illuminator of Knowledge will pass by in great glory," Adam continues. "And he will perform signs and wonders in order to scorn the powers and their ruler. Then the god of the powers will be disturbed, saying 'What is the power of this man who is higher than we?' Then he will arouse a great wrath against that man. And the glory will withdraw and dwell in holy houses, which it has chosen for itself. And the powers will not see it with their eyes, nor will they see the Illuminator, either. Then they will punish the flesh of the man upon whom the Holy Spirit came."

This is a familiar Gnostic theme, the idea of a cruel and jealous Creator God who cannot abide the superior knowledge of his creation. While the Illuminator attains a more perfect knowledge of himself, he is nevertheless vulnerable to punishment from the "powers," though that punishment is never explicitly named in the book, and is too vague to be taken as a literal description of the crucifixion. Also, this is supposed to be the third appearance of the Illuminator, which does not correspond to any recognizable Jewish or Christian prophecy of the messiah. Are we perhaps dealing with the third lifetime of a soul previously made incarnate as another entity altogether?

THE BIRTH OF THE ILLUMINATOR

Therefore it has been proposed that the Illuminator is an embodiment of Gnostic ideals separate from the gospel Jesus. The Apocalypse of Adam also describes a series of thirteen false birth legends, including several versions of a virgin birth, on its way to declaring the true origins of the Illuminator.

The first legend, for instance, claims that the Illuminator was nourished in the heavens, received glory and power and then came to the bosom of his mother. The second legend says that he came from a great prophet, and that he was taken by a bird to a high mountain and was nourished there, until an angel came and gave the Illuminator glory and strength. The third legend says he came from a virgin womb, was cast out of his city along with his mother, and brought to a desert place where he again is nourished and receives glory and power.

The fourth legend claims that Solomon sent his "army of demons" to seek out the virgin. Solomon took her and the virgin became pregnant. After the child is born, his mother nourishes him in the desert, and he is given glory and power. The fifth legend declares that the Illuminator was dropped down from heaven, then thrown into the sea, where the abyss received him, gave birth to him, and returned him to heaven.

The sixth legend says that the mother came down from on high to pick flowers, and those same flowers impregnated her. She gave birth to the Illuminator, and the angels of the flower garden nourished him. A seventh legend tells the story of the Illuminator being dropped from heaven again, but this time the child is brought by dragons to a network of caves, before he is returned to heaven as in the earlier legend.

Birth legend number eight has the Illuminator created when a cloud comes upon the earth and envelopes a rock. "The angels who were above the cloud nourished him." The ninth legend says that one of the nine Muses separated from the others and went to sit on a mountain. The lone Muse wishes to become androgynous, which she manages to accomplish, even becoming pregnant by herself. The Illuminator is born, and is again nourished by angels.

The tenth legend credits the Illuminator's birth to a god who loved a cloud of desire, and begets the Illuminator "in his hand, and cast upon the cloud above him some of the drop, and he was born." The eleventh legend has the Illuminator born by an incestuous relationship between a father and his daughter. The woman is cast out into the desert, where an angel nourishes the child. The twelfth legend says the Illuminator was born from two other Illuminators, while the thirteenth legend cryptically reads as, "Every birth of their ruler is a word. And his word received a mandate there. He received glory and power in order that the desire of those powers might be satisfied."

THE BATTLE CRY OF TRUTH

And those are just the legends that got it wrong. According to the Apocalypse of Adam, this is the real truth:

"But the generation with no king over it says that God chose him . . . . He caused knowledge of the undefiled one of truth to come to be in him. He said, 'Out of a foreign air, the great Illuminator came forth. And he made the generation of those men whom he had chosen for himself shine.'

"Then the seed, those who will receive his name upon the water, will fight against the power. And a cloud of darkness will come upon them. Then the peoples will cry out with a great voice, saying 'Blessed is the soul of those men because they have known God with a knowledge of the truth! They shall live forever; because they have not been corrupted by their desire, along with the angels, nor have they accomplished the works of the powers, but have stood in his presence in a knowledge of God like light that has come forth from fire and blood.'"

Again, understanding all of this involves some rather tricky inversions of the usual account of Adam and the fall from grace. Adam refers to his creator as "the god of the powers," whom he serves in fear and slavery. Meanwhile, in the verses above, the Illuminator and his seed are sent to do battle with those same powers, the creator god who cast Adam out of paradise when he learned the "word of knowledge of the eternal God" from Eve. This is a familiar element of the excluded books of the Bible. There are also several other Gnostic books in which the creator of the physical world is perceived as the true source of evil, and man must seek deliverance from him by appealing to something higher, which in this case is the prophesied coming of a messiah called the Illuminator.

After being chosen by the true God who dwells far above the creator-of-the-powers physical reality, the Illuminator will do battle with the lower god and win a great victory for the enlightened who believe in a transcendent form of reality.

Adam then confesses our unworthiness of this coming messiah.

"But we have done every deed of the powers senselessly. We have boasted in the transgression of all our works. These are against our spirits. For now we have known that our souls will die a death."

Yet deliverance will come, Adam says, and angels will bring the faithful to a high mountain, a rock of truth.

"Therefore they will be named 'The Words of Imperishability and Truth,' for those who know the eternal God in wisdom of knowledge and teachings of angels forever, for he knows all things."

AN UNDERSTANDABLE ATTITUDE

The Apocalypse of Adam concludes by saying that these are things that Adam revealed to Seth, who in turn passed them on to his descendants: the "holy baptism of those who know the eternal knowledge through those born of the word and the imperishable illuminators, who came from the holy seed."

The perspective that the Gnostics had developed toward the evil and corruption of the physical world is understandable. Just as there are those who say they cannot imagine a benevolent Creator who would have made such misery and pain and therefore cannot believe in God at all, so the Gnostics sometimes blamed creation on an evil, jealous, violent and wrathful God who had no love in his heart for the people and things he had made to dwell below him. The Gnostics, however, then appeal to a higher court, as it were, to a God who shines above the one who merely "created" man's sorry and miserable lot. This truly benevolent higher God then sends his servant the Illuminator to deliver us from our error and delusion.

It's always good to have that little escape clause, isn't it? Especially after condemning the whole of creation as a vile and unworthy corpse whom we have inevitably served.

Chapter Seven
Ascension Through The Heavens

- Read about the strange journey of the Apostle Paul through the ten levels of heaven, where he sees such visions as angels whipping a soul from the land of the dead.
- Who is the "toll-collector," and what role does he play in heavenly affairs?
- Is our image of a white-haired Yahweh sitting on his throne of glory a mistake that has been carried down through the millennia? Is that familiar picture of Yahweh really an illusion created for the sake of enslaving mankind to a lesser God?

With a book from the Nag Hammadi find called the Apocalypse of Paul, we have an excellent example of typical Gnostic beliefs. The very short book tells the story of Saint Paul's journey through the ten levels of heaven, past an angry and judgmental Yahweh and up to a lofty position where he meets the other apostles in spirit form.

Paul's journey begins on the road to Jerusalem, where he meets a small child.

"I know who you are, Paul," the child tells him. "You are he who was blessed from his mother's womb. For I have come to you that you may go up to Jerusalem to your fellow apostles. And for this reason you were called. And I am the spirit who accompanies you.

"Let your mind awaken, Paul," the child/spirit continues, "and see that this mountain upon which you are standing is the mountain of Jericho, so that you may know the hidden things in those that are visible. Now it is to the twelve apostles that you shall go, for they are elect spirits, and they will greet you."

Paul raises his eyes and does indeed see the apostles greeting him.

"Then the Holy Spirit who was speaking with him caught him up on high to the third heaven, and he passed beyond to the fourth heaven. The Holy Spirit spoke to him saying, 'Look and see your likeness upon the earth.' And he looked down and saw those who were upon the earth. Then he gazed down and saw the twelve apostles at his right hand and at his left in the creation, and the Spirit was going before him."

A SOUL TAKES A BEATING

In that fourth heaven, Paul sees a strange sight indeed, one not cataloged in the traditional holy books.

"I saw the angels," Paul reports, "resembling gods, the angels bringing a soul out of the land of the dead. They placed it at the gate of the fourth heaven. And the angels were whipping it."

The soul opens his mouth to protest, saying, "What sin was it that I committed in the world?"

The reply comes from an entity Paul spookily enough calls "the toll-collector."

"It was not right to commit all those lawless deeds," the toll-collector says to the soul, "that are in the world of the dead."

The soul continues to contend, saying, "Bring witnesses! Let them show you in what body I committed lawless deeds. Do you wish to bring a book to read from?"

Three witnesses appear and begin to testify against the soul.

"The first spoke, saying, 'Was I not in the body the second hour? I rose up against you until you fell into anger and rage and envy.' And the second spoke, saying, 'Was I not in the world? And I entered at the fifth hour, and I saw you and desired you. And behold, then, now I charge you with the murders you committed.' The third spoke, saying, 'Did I not come to you at the twelfth hour of the day when the sun was about to set? I gave you darkness until you should accomplish your sins.'

"When the soul heard these things, it gazed downward in sorrow. And then it gazed upward. It was cast down. The soul that had been cast down went to a body which had been prepared for it. And behold, its witnesses were finished."

DRIVEN BY WHIPS

After witnessing this strange and sorrowful scene, the Holy Spirit then leads Paul further onward.

"Then as I went, the gate opened and I went up to the fifth heaven," Paul says. "And I saw my fellow apostles going with me while the Spirit accompanied us. And I saw a great angel in the fifth heaven holding an iron rod in his hand. There were three other angels with him, and I stared into their faces. But they were rivaling each other, with whips in their hands, goading the souls on to judgment. But I went with the Spirit, and the gate opened for me."

Again with the whips! As far as tours of heaven go, this one is certainly a little different.

"Then we went up to the sixth heaven," Paul goes on. "And I saw my fellow apostles going with me, and the Holy Spirit was leading me before them. And I gazed up on high and saw a great light shining down on the sixth heaven. I spoke, saying to the toll-collector who was in the sixth heaven, 'Open to me and the Holy Spirit who is before me.' He opened to me."

MEETING A NEGATIVE VERSION OF GOD

The seventh heaven is quite problematic for those who believe in a great bearded Yahweh sitting on his throne. Here Paul encounters that type of depiction of God, but the meeting is not a pleasant one.

"Then we went up to the seventh heaven," Paul says, "and I saw an old man whose garment was white. His throne, which is in the seventh heaven, was brighter than the sun by seven times. The old man spoke, saying to me, 'Where are you going Paul, O blessed one and the one who was set apart from his mother's womb?' But I looked at the Spirit, and he was nodding his head, saying to me, 'Speak with him!'

"And I replied, saying to the old man, 'I am going to the place from which I came.' And the old man responded to me, 'Where are you from?' But I replied, saying, 'I am going down to the world of the dead in order to lead captive the captivity that was led captive in the captivity of Babylon.' The old man replied to me, saying, 'How will you be able to get away from me? Look and see the principalities and authorities.' The Spirit spoke, saying, 'Give him the sign that you have and he will open for you.' And I gave him the sign. He turned his face downwards to his creation, and to those who are his own authorities."

Once again we are confronted with a very negative portrayal of the Creator God of the Bible. Here he attempts to block Paul's further ascension into the heavens, even seeming to mock Paul's blessed status among his fellow mortals as he threatens not to let the sojourner pass by. As has been noted previously, the Gnostics often despised the suffering and corruption of the physical world, and therefore characterized he who created it as evil.

The Apocalypse of Paul ends with a brief description of the passage through heavens eight, nine and ten. At the end, Paul has become a spirit form himself, and joins his fellow apostles in the tenth heaven as a creature transformed.

Chapter Eight
Jesus In Disguise

- Did Jesus change his physical appearance from time to time in order to teach his disciples about the Kingdom of Heaven?
- Who was the pearl salesman that Saint Peter encountered in the small town called Habitation?
- Why did the accounts of John and James differ so widely from one another when they spoke of how Jesus appeared to them? Was Jesus old or young, flesh or spirit?

The Acts of Peter and the Twelve Apostles is set in the times after the crucifixion and resurrection and opens as the disciples converse among themselves about how to do the will of Jesus in his absence.

"We agreed to fulfill the ministry to which the Lord appointed us," Peter says. "And we made a covenant with each other."

Peter and the others go down to the sea "at an opportune moment, which came to us from the Lord. We found a ship moored at the shore ready to embark, and we spoke with the sailors of the ship about our coming aboard with them. They showed great kindliness toward us, as was ordained by the Lord."

PETER LAYS EYES ON A MYSTERIOUS STRANGER

The disciples sail for a day and a night. A wind comes up and brings them to a small city in the midst of the sea. Peter asks one of the locals what the city is called, and is told the city's name is Habitation. The disciples bring their baggage ashore and Peter sets out to find lodgings for them all.

As he seeks shelter for the group, Peter sees a man "wearing a cloth bound around his waist, and a gold belt girded it. Also a napkin was tied over his chest, extending over his shoulders and covering his head and his hands."

Peter finds himself staring at the man "because he was beautiful in his form and stature. There were four parts of his body that I saw: the soles of his feet and a part of his chest and the palms of his hands and his visage. These things I was able to see. His voice was resounding as he spoke, crying out in the city, 'Pearls! Pearls!'"

Thinking the man is just another resident of the city, Peter approaches him, saying, "My brother and my friend." The man answers, saying, "Rightly did you say, 'My brother and my friend.' What is it you seek from me?"

Peter informs the pearl salesman that he seeks lodging for himself and the other disciples. The man then tells Peter that he also is a stranger in town, and resumes his shouting of the word "Pearls!"

The rich men of the city disdain the pearl salesman, seeing that he is dressed poorly and does not carry a pouch on his back to bear his goods with. They do not acknowledge him, and he does not reveal himself to them, either.

But the poor of the city hear his voice and approach him, asking that he simply show them the pearl, "so that we may see it with our own eyes. For we are the poor, and we do not have this price to pay for it. But show us that we might say to our friends that we saw a pearl with our own eyes."

The pearl salesman answers them, saying, "If it is possible, come to my city, so that I may not only show it before your very eyes, but give it to you for nothing."

The poor respond by saying that it is more often food or money that is given to the poor, not pearls. The pearl salesman repeats his offer of a free pearl if they will come to his city, and this time the poor rejoice at the news.

Peter, who has been seeing all this unfold, asks the pearl salesman what his name is.

"If you seek my name," the salesman replies, "Lithargoel is my name, the interpretation of which is 'the light, gazelle-like stone.'"

THE DANGEROUS JOURNEY

Peter asks further about the hardships of the journey to Lithargoel's city, and receives this reply: "No man is able to go on that road except one who has forsaken everything that he has and has fasted daily from stage to stage. For many are the robbers and the wild beasts on that road. The one who carries bread with him on the road, the black dogs will kill because of the bread. The one who carries a costly garment of the world with him, the robbers will kill because of the garment. The one who carries water with him, the wolves will kill because of the water, since they are thirsty for it. The one who is anxious about meat and green vegetables, the lions eat because of the meat. If he evades the lions, the bulls devour him because of the green vegetables."

Peter sighs within himself, saying the hardships the pearl salesman describes sound terrible.

"If only Jesus would give us the power to walk it!"

The pearl salesman studies Peter's sad face and says to him, "Why do you sigh, if you, indeed, know this name 'Jesus' and believe him? He is a great power for giving strength. For I too believe in the Father who sent him."

After saying goodbye to the pearl salesman, Peter next sees a vision of the city with high walls of water all around it. He asks the name of the city and is again told it is called Habitation. Peter returns to the disciples with the idea in mind of journeying to the city of the pearl salesman, which is called "Nine Gates." They agree to travel with nothing, as the pearl salesman had advised them, so that they would not be robbed on the road by the various thieves Peter had been warned about.

A spirit of great joy comes upon Peter and the others as they discuss successfully evading the many thieves who might have harmed them. At which point, Lithargoel, the pearl salesman, comes to the group, his appearance now changed to that of a physician, with an unguent box under his arm and a young disciple following him with a pouch of medicine. The disciples do not recognize him.

Peter asks the physician for directions to Lithargoel's house, and the physician replies, "In uprightness of heart I will show it to you. But I am amazed at how you knew this good man. For he does not reveal himself to every man, because he himself is the son of a great king. Rest yourselves a little so that I may go and heal this man and come back."

The physician hurries back to the group and calls Peter by name, which frightens Peter since no one has told the physician who Peter is.

THE TRUE IDENTITY REVEALED

The physician, who is also Lithargoel the pearl salesman, then reveals himself as Christ the Lord. The disciples prostrate themselves in worship and swear to do the will of Jesus. Jesus tells them to return to the city of Habitation and preach to the poor and give them what they need. Having renounced all worldly goods, however, Peter protests that they now have nothing to give the poor.

"The Lord answered and said, 'O Peter, it was necessary that you understand the parable that I told you! Do you not understand that my name, which you teach, surpasses all riches, and the wisdom of God surpasses gold and silver and precious stones?'"

Jesus then gives them his pouch of medicine and instructs them to heal all the sick of the city. Peter is too choked up to continue the conversation, and asks the disciple John to speak instead. John then asks Jesus how they can be expected to heal without being taught to be physicians.

Jesus replies, "Rightly have you spoken, John, for I know that the physicians of this world heal what belongs to the world. The physicians of souls, however, heal the heart. Heal the bodies first, therefore, so that through the real powers of healing for their bodies, without medicine of the world, they may believe in you, that you have power to heal the illnesses of the heart also."

The disciples are then instructed to disdain the rich and not to dine in their houses nor be friends with them, "lest their partiality influence you." The disciples answer Jesus by saying, "Yes, truly this is what is fitting to do." They again prostrate themselves before Jesus, who "caused them to stand and departed from them in peace."

THE CHANGING FACE OF JESUS

The Acts of Peter and the Twelve Apostles offers a fascinating account of Jesus in his many guises, and begs comparison to the late scholar of myth Joseph Campbell's four-part work, *The Masks of God*. There is no one face or personality for the Jesus described here, but instead a series of incarnations and embodiments that each serve a different purpose and lead the believer from one point of revelation to another, the various "masks" of the deity.

In part three of the *Masks of God*, entitled *Occidental Mythology*, Campbell relates another story of Jesus in disguise from the Gnostic book the Acts of John.

"The Messiah has just come from his desert fast of forty days," Campbell writes, setting the scene, "and his victory there over Satan. John and James are in their boat, fishing. Christ appears on the shore. And John is supposed to be telling, now, of the occasion."

The scripture commences.

"For when he had chosen Peter and Andrew, who were brothers, he came to me and James my brother, saying, 'I have need of you, come unto me.' And my brother, hearing that, said to me, 'John, what does that child want who is on the shore there and called to us?' And I said, 'What child?' And he said again, 'The one beckoning to us.' And I answered, 'Because of the long watch we have kept at sea, you are not seeing right, my brother James. But do you not see the man who is standing there, comely, fair, and of cheerful countenance?' But he answered, 'Him, brother, I do not see. But let us go and we shall see what he wants.'

"And so, when we had brought our boat to land, we saw him also, helping us to settle it; and when we had left, thinking to follow him, he appeared to me to be rather bald, but with a beard thick and flowing, but to James he seemed a youth whose beard had newly come. We were therefore, both of us, perplexed as to what we had seen should mean. And as we followed him, continuing, we both were, little by little, even more perplexed as we considered the matter. For in my case, there appeared this still more wonderful thing: I would try to watch him secretly, and I never at any time saw his eyes blinking, but only open. And often he would appear to me to be a little man, uncomely, but then again as one reaching up to heaven. Moreover, there was in him another marvel: when we sat to eat he would clasp me   to his breast, and sometimes the breast felt to me to be smooth and tender, but sometimes hard like stone.

"Another glory, also, would I tell to you, my brethren: namely, that sometimes when I would take hold of him, I would meet with a material and solid body, but again, at other times, when I touched him, the substance was immaterial and as if it existed not at all. And if at any time he were invited by some Pharisee and accepted the invitation, we accompanied him; and there was set before each of us a loaf by those who entertained; and with us, he too received one. But his own he would bless and apportion among us. And of that little, every one was filled, and our own loaves were saved whole, so that those who had invited him were amazed. And often, when I walked with him, I desired to see the print of his foot, whether it appeared on the earth; for I saw him, as it were, sustaining himself above the earth; and I never saw it.

"And these things I tell you, my brethren, for the encouragement of your faith in him; for we must, at present, keep silence concerning his mighty and wonderful works, in as much as they are unspeakable, and, it may be, cannot at all be uttered or be heard."

Campbell then explains that this ancient view of Jesus holds that Christ's body, as seen by men, was "a mere appearance, the reality being celestial or divine, and its appearance furthermore, a function of the mentality of the seer, not of the reality of the seen; a mere mask that might change but not be removed."

The face and body of Jesus could be anything, anywhere and anyone. It is understandable that the orthodox hierarchy would reject such a view of Jesus. A carefully choreographed game of "Now you see him, now you don't" is a hard and elusive thing to grasp even in this supposedly more enlightened age, and a Jesus with a perpetually changing face doesn't exactly fit one's notion of "that old-time religion," does it? But it is an enthralling mystery nevertheless, and one worthy of continued contemplation by those seek a truth not often told in the mainstream churches of our time.

Chapter Nine
The Traitor's Story

- Read about the flurry of opinions in the wake of the recent discovery of a Gnostic book called The Gospel of Judas. Will it change how the Orthodox Church views the story of Christ's betrayer?

- Should we modify our traditional point of view to include the idea that even the evil figures in the Bible, such as Judas and Cain, were really carrying out the will of God?

- Did Jesus convince Judas to betray him in order to that Jesus' mission to die on the cross could be carried out?

In the years since the Nag Hammadi find in 1945, a newly discovered Gnostic book has been translated. Called The Gospel of Judas, it may threaten to change completely the ancient story of Jesus' betrayal by his disciple Judas.

THE JUDAS WE ALL KNEW AND HATED

"About 2000 years after the Gospel of Judas sowed discord among early Christians," says an online report from March of 2005, "a Swiss foundation says it is translating for the first time the controversial text named after the apostle said to have betrayed Jesus Christ. The 62-page papyrus of the text was uncovered in Egypt during the 1950s or 1960s, but its owners did not fully comprehend its significance until recently, according to the Maecenas Foundation in Basle."

A more recent report from the British newspaper "The Telegraph" says, "Although the details have not yet been made public, snippets discussed in academic circles say it will prove Judas was acting at the behest of God when he sold Jesus to the Romans for 30 pieces of silver. Its publication will raise fears among traditionalists that efforts may be made to rehabilitate a man whose name is synonymous with betrayal. Sympathizers with Judas contend that had Jesus not been crucified, he would not have been subsequently resurrected to save humanity."

The Reuters News Service summarized the reputation of Judas this way: "The name Judas, his reward of 30 pieces of silver and the kiss he gave to Jesus to identify him to Roman soldiers have been symbols of treachery in Western culture for two millennia. In 'Dante's Inferno,' he languishes in the lowest circle of Hell.

"But the disgraced apostle raises a difficult question for theologians," the Reuters report continues. "If Jesus was supposed to die on the cross as part of a larger divine plan, did Judas not simply play a his part in the drama by turning him over to the Roman occupiers? And is Christianity not supposed to be about forgiveness?"

THE POPE TO BLESS JUDAS?

There had even been speculation that the Vatican was going to go public with some sort of vindication of the role of Judas in the passion of Christ.

"This news has no foundation," says Walter Brandmueller, head of the Pontifical Committee of Historical Sciences. "I can't imagine where this idea came from."

One possible source of that idea may lie in the fact that putting Judas in a more favorable light would alleviate Vatican relations with Judaism, since anti-Semites sometimes use his story to condemn all Jews.

"The dialogue between the Holy See and the Jews continues profitably on other bases," Brandmueller said in reply.

THE DOCUMENT ITSELF

According to the Telegraph article, the translator of the Gospel of Judas is Rodolphe Kasser of the University of Geneva, considered the world's greatest Coptic Scholar. Coptic is the language the new gospel is written in, as is true of the Gnostic books found at Nag Hammadi.

"The torn and tattered papyrus text had been offered to potential buyers in North America and Europe for decades after it was found at al-Minya in Egypt. It resurfaced recently as the property of the Maecenas Foundation based in Basle, Switzerland."

While it remains a point of controversy as to who actually wrote the gospel, most scholars believe it was not written by the actual historical Judas but rather by a group of his supporters. Scholars are also in agreement that it was most likely written in Greek in the second century A.D., with the scribal hand that copied and preserved the document dating to around the fourth or fifth century.

Charles Hendrick, recently retired from Missouri State University, has seen photographs of six damaged pages of the document.

"I don't think it will unsettle the church," he said. "I mean we are not talking history here. We know very little about Judas from the New Testament and some people have even challenged whether Judas was an historical person."

The 62 pages of Coptic Texts also contain the The First Apocalypse of James and the Letter of Peter To Philip, both of which were also part of the Gnostic scriptures found at Nag Hammadi.

Hedrick says the last six pages of the Judas document describe "a heavenly scene in which Allogenes is being tested and tried by Satan, followed by an earthly scene in which Jesus is being closely watched by scribes. At one point, Judas is told, 'Although you are evil at this place, you are a disciple of Jesus.' The last line of the text says, 'And Judas took money and delivered Jesus over.'"

Which makes it appear, Hedrick says, "that Judas is working at the behest of God when he betrays Jesus as part of the divine plan."

But Hedrick thinks that public interest in the Judas Gospel will be short-lived, and any sensationalism caused by the translation and analyses will dribble out, leaving only scholars interested.

SHIFTS IN THE NATURE OF TRUTH

Still, that excitement among scholars may last for many years, since the discovery touches not only on Coptic, Gnostic and apocryphal studies, but also on studies of ancient Judaism and Christianity. There is some discussion underway as to whether the document was produced by a branch of Gnostics called "Cainites" by church leaders. The Cainites were said to have glorified Cain and other disgraced figures in the Bible because, according to Gnostic viewpoints, they were doing God's work.

The Telegraph report continues: "Church discussions conceivably could revolve around the extent to which New Testament Gospels present events in Jesus' life and passion as ordained from the start. Judas Iscariot, depicted minimally by the Gospel of Mark, received elaboration in Matthew, Luke and John. The latter Gospel says Satan entered Judas at the Last Supper just before Jesus told the disciple, 'Do quickly what you are going to do.'"

But how much will our understanding of the truth really change as a result of the Gospel of Judas?

One scholar not clearly identified in the Telegraph article half jokingly said, "Where would Christianity be, if there had been no Judas, and Jesus—instead of dying for our sins on the cross—had died of old age? So thank God for Judas? Even the most broadminded among us would call that heresy."

It should be pointed out that this is exactly the scenario depicted in the 1988 Martin Scorsese blockbuster "The Last Temptation of Christ." In the final scenes of the movie, as Christ is in his delirium of pain on the cross, Judas, as played by actor Harvey Keitel, stands before Willem Dafoe as Jesus and says accusingly that Jesus had failed to do as he had promised when he had convinced Judas to betray him. The idea that Jesus had secretly conspired with Judas in order to guarantee his execution by the Romans is not totally new, as the movie bears witness, but has been passed down from a group of ancients who chose to differ with the New Testament portrayal of Judas as acting on his own and/or at Satan's behest.

Will it ever be possible to uncover what we might loosely call "the facts" in the story of Judas as the betrayer of Christ? It has been said more than once that the authors of these ancient books, both the Gnostic and the canonical writers, were in no way attempting to write "journalistic" accounts of the story of Jesus. They were instead writing symbolic stories intended for a select audience of fellow believers who were already predisposed, for the most part, to take what they were reading as the "gospel truth." Until such time as the truth is finally unveiled, until some revelation is made that we cannot even conceive of presently, we must be content with different warring versions of the truth in which one scholar's word is as good as another's.

Chapter Ten
Was The Resurrection For Real?

- What portions of ourselves will survive after death? Will we leave our thoughts and consciousness behind on earth?
- Is there a new, glorified body in our future when we die? What kind of physical transformation should we look forward to?
- Is the material world itself an illusion? Is the life of the spirit the true reality?

There are many differing views of the resurrection of Jesus Christ and what it implies for believers. For instance, present day Jehovah's Witnesses believe the resurrection was a spiritual one, and not intended to be seen as a literal physical resurrection of Christ's fleshly body. A similar controversy raged during the days when the Gnostic scriptures were written, and a very short book called The Treatise On The Resurrection attempted to provide answers to its Gnostic community of readers.

DEATH IS VANQUISHED

The Treatise On The Resurrection is in the form of a letter written in support of a distinctly unorthodox view of survival after death. It asks the question, "How did the Lord proclaim things while he existed in flesh and after he had revealed himself as Son of God? He lived in this place where you remain, speaking about the Law of Nature— but I call it 'Death!'"

Which is to say that the physical world is actually the domain of death, which Christ was sent to vanquish through his dual identity as both Son of God and Son of Man.

"The Savior swallowed up death," the book continues, "for he put aside the world, which is perishing. He transformed himself into an imperishable heavenly power, and raised himself up, having swallowed the visible by the invisible, and he gave us the way of immortality."

As we share in the suffering of Christ, we also share in his resurrection.

"Then indeed, as the Apostle said, 'We suffered with him, and we arose with him, and we went to heaven with him.' Now, if we are manifest in this world wearing him, we are one another's beams, and we are embraced with him until our setting, that is to say our death in this life. We are drawn to heaven by him, like beams by the sun, not being restrained by anything. This is the spiritual resurrection, which swallows up the psychic in the same way as the fleshly."

The letter next declares that these are matters of faith, and not of persuasive argument, that the dead shall rise.

"For we have known the Son of Man, and we have believed that he rose from among the dead. This is he of whom we say, 'He became the destruction of death, as he is a great one in whom they believe.' Great are those who believe."

WILL WE STILL BE OUR TRUE SELVES?

The letter also promises that we will survive with our thoughts and consciousness—the elements that compose our earthly identity—intact.

"The thought of those who are saved shall not perish. The mind of those who have known him shall not perish. Therefore we are elected to salvation and redemption since we are predestined from the beginning not to fall into the foolishness of those who are without knowledge, but we shall enter into the wisdom of those who have known the Truth. Indeed, the Truth which is kept cannot be abandoned, nor has it been."

This last section states one of the primary tenets of Gnostic belief, that a primal form of Truth, of secret knowledge available only to believers, of "gnosis," is necessary for genuine salvation. It also has echoes of the mainstream New Testament belief that those who attain salvation were predestined to do so, especially as argued for by Saint Paul.

The Treatise On the Resurrection also talks of the believer receiving a new body after death.

"For if you were not existing in the flesh, you received flesh when you entered this world. Why will you not receive flesh when you ascend into the heavenly places? The afterbirth of the body is old age, and you exist in corruption. For you will not give up what is better if you depart."

There is a further attempt on the part of the author to clarify what he means.

"But there are some who wish to understand, in the enquiry about those things they are looking into, whether he who is saved, if he leaves his body behind, will be saved immediately. Let no one doubt concerning this. Indeed, the visible members, which are dead, shall not be saved, for only the living members which exist within them would arise."

The issue remains a little muddled, however, but the author seems to be restating the idea that the flesh of believer will be changed to some glorious new form, which will be brought to life with the inner-self unchanged.

IT'S THE WORLD THAT ISN'T REAL

The author points to the New Testament story of the Transfiguration, when Moses and Elijah appear next to Jesus, cautioning that no one should condemn the moment as just an illusion.

"It is no illusion, but it is truth! Indeed, it is more fitting to say that the world is an illusion, rather than the resurrection which has come into being through our Lord and Savior, Jesus Christ."

There shall also come a form of judgment for those who live in illusion.

"The rich have become poor, and the kings have been overthrown. Everything is prone to change. The world is an illusion!"

But the resurrection stands firm through changing times.

"It is the revelation of what is, and the transformation of things, and a transition into newness. For imperishability descends upon the perishable, the light flows down on the darkness, swallowing it up. These are the symbols and the images of the resurrection. Christ it is who makes the good."

The author next argues that one can view oneself as already living in the resurrection.

"For if he who will die knows about himself that he will die—even if he spend many years in this life, he is brought to this—why not consider yourself as risen and already brought to this?"

In other words, knowing that we shall one day die, can we not equally know we shall one day be resurrected and so believe and act accordingly, as one already saved?

The Treatise On The Resurrection concludes by saying that the message contained here was received directly from Jesus Christ and that the author will be happy to try and make plain what his readers may yet find obscure.

"Many are looking into this which I have written you. To these I say: peace be among them and grace. I greet you and those who love you in brotherly love."

That final paragraph seems to indicate a kind of foreknowledge on the part of the author, as though he knew his words would be scrutinized not only by the people of his time, but also by a future audience who would come much later to study closely what he had to say. Whether he was actually prescient in those terms or not, he did indeed find a 21st century audience for his preaching concerning the true nature of the resurrection, an audience that continues to hunger after many of the same truths.

Chapter Eleven
A Strange Trip Into The Mind Of Jesus

- Can we imagine an imperfect Jesus, one riddled with self-doubt and ignorant of his own nature?
- Was Jesus subject to the same spiritual dangers as everybody else? Read about his narrow escape from an evil fate.
- Did Jesus come packaged with spirits in his eyes and ears who helped him function as the savior?

Gnostic scripture often dares to be different, which is an obvious reason for it being excluded from the Bible as we know it. In a somewhat lengthy book discovered at Nag Hammadi, called The Tripartite Tractate, the reader is taken on a strange journey into the mind of Jesus that starts with his creation and then moves on through to the inner workings of his mind as he discovers his identity and powers.

THE NATURE OF THE FATHER

The Tripartite Tractate begins with a description of the Father who begat Jesus, saying, "Not only is he the one called 'without a beginning,' and 'without an end,' because he is unbegotten and immortal; but just as he has no beginning and no end, as he is, he is unattainable in his greatness, inscrutable in his wisdom, incomprehensible in his power, and unfathomable in his sweetness.

"In the proper sense, he alone, the good, the unbegotten Father and the complete perfect one, is the one filled with all his offspring and with every virtue and with everything of value. And he has more, that is, lack of any malice, in order that it may be discovered that whoever has anything is indebted to him, because he gives it, being himself unreachable and unwearied by that which he gives, since he is wealthy in the gifts that he bestows and at rest in the favors which he grants.

"He is of such a kind and form and great magnitude that no one else has been with him from the beginning; nor is there a place in which he is, or from which he has come forth, or into which he will go; nor is there a primordial form, which he uses as a model as he works; nor is there any difficulty which accompanies him in what he does; nor is there any material which is at his disposal, from which he creates what he creates; nor any substance within him from which he begets what he begets; nor a coworker with him, working with him on the things at which he works. To say anything of this sort is ignorant. Rather, one should speak of him as good, faultless, perfect, complete, being himself the Totality."

Scholars recognize this pattern of description as something called a "via negativa," which means that God is described mostly by saying what he is not rather than as a description of what he is. The list of negative statements in the preceding quotes therefore describe one transcendent of any of our normal assumptions of what the original consciousness actually "is."

THE CREATION OF THE SON

After listing the attributes of the Father, The Tripartite Tractate moves on to describe the creation of the Son, who also has none other like him

"Just as the Father exists in the perfect sense, the one before whom there was no one else and the one apart from whom there is no other unbegotten one, so too the Son exists in the proper sense, the one before whom there was no other, and after whom no other son exists. Therefore he is a firstborn and an only Son, 'firstborn' because no one exists before him and 'only Son' because no one is after him. Furthermore, he has his fruit, that which is unknowable because of its surpassing greatness. Yet he wanted it to be known, because of the riches of his sweetness. And he revealed the unexplainable power and he combined it with the great abundance of his generosity."

This is a description of Jesus in the earliest stages of his existence, and it states quite clearly that Jesus will have none other like him either before or after his creation.

Further along in The Tripartite Tractate, Jesus is called by the name "the Logos," or the Divine Word, as he is called in the Gospel of John from the New Testament.

When the Logos comes to look upon the light, he is deeply troubled, and turned away "because of his self-doubt and division, forgetfulness and ignorance of himself and of that which is. His self-exaltation and his expectation of comprehending the incomprehensible became firm for him and was in him. But the sicknesses followed him when he went beyond himself, having come into being from self-doubt, namely from the fact that he did not reach the attainment of the glories of the Father, the one whose exalted status is among things unlimited. This one did not attain him, for he did not receive him."

This is a rather complex inventory of what might loosely be called "the sick mind of Jesus." In his early stages of development, in some kind of spiritual limbo often called "pre-history," he is said to be ignorant of his own nature, and forgetful of what he has been taught about himself. Part of this sickness is caused by self-doubt, but another part is caused by Jesus assuming that he can comprehend what is for him incomprehensible, and by aspiring to reach the level of the Father, which is impossible as well.

When, a short time later, Jesus is also said to have become "weak, like a female nature which has abandoned its virile counterpart," are we to believe that Jesus was for a time effeminate? Even that he needs a special deliverance from his own arrogance, as is stated in the verses just following? This is apparently not about a Jesus that we could literally call perfect. Instead, he seems to have a great many personal problems on his way to an illumined realization of his own identity as the Son of God.

THE IMPERFECT CREATIONS OF JESUS

In spite of what can be considered an impaired mental state, Jesus also has the power to create things simply by thinking about them. But his initial creations are to say the least imperfect.

"Like the holy things are the things that came into being from the arrogant thought, which are their likenesses, copies, shadows and phantasms, lacking reason and the light, these which belong to the vain thought, since they are not products of anything. Therefore their end will be like their beginning: from that which did not exist they are to return once again to that which will not be."

Since these imperfect creations, or likenesses, are not aware of the limits of their own existence, they live in disobedience and rebellion, without having humbled themselves to the Son who created them.

"They are likenesses of the things which are exalted. They were brought to a lust for power in each one of them, according to the greatness of the name of which each is a shadow, each one imagining that it is superior to his fellows. Therefore it happened that many offspring came forth from them, as fighters, as warriors, as troublemakers, as apostates. They are disobedient beings, lovers of power. All the other beings of this sort were brought forth from these."

Jesus, as Logos, is charged with introducing rebellious, evil entities on the world, which causes him "to be at a loss, and he was astonished. Instead of perfection, he saw a defect; instead of unification, he saw division; instead of stability, he saw disturbances; instead of rests, tumults. Neither was it possible for him to make them cease from loving disturbance, nor was it possible for him to destroy it. He was completely powerless, once his totality and his exaltation abandoned him."

This is indeed quite a different version of Jesus, isn't it? Did we ever before think he might be "at a loss," or "completely powerless"?

Suffering as he is from confusion and weakness, his thoughts next bring forth not the powerful emanations of heaven that he is capable of, but instead "little weaklings, hindered by the illnesses by which he too is hindered."

THE LOGOS IS CONVERTED

Having seen the wicked and weak things he has begotten, the Logos "turned to another opinion and another thought. Having turned away from evil, he turned toward the good things. Following the conversion came the thought of the things which exist and the prayer for the one who converted himself to the good."

It is through that prayer that the Logos is helped to return to the Father, the good powers that are greater than the falsely created "likenesses." But isn't it interesting that we seem to be hearing about a spiritual crisis experienced by Jesus himself, a painful learning experience that would have dragged him down even unto hell had he not somehow righted himself and been restored to his Father/creator. There are spiritual dangers lurking in the shadows even for Jesus, which can be quite an encouraging thought for the rest of us if we approach it in the right way.

THE SPIRITS SENT TO HELP JESUS

Along with his spiritual conversion to obedience to the Father, there is also an attribute given to him, some kind of mental aid called "the beings of thought," with whom Jesus is apparently quite content. Could these beings of thought be voices in the mind, something similar to what schizophrenics or clairaudients hear? One would think that in the case of Jesus these voices might actually be helpful, and might form a working unit in combination with the more mortal Son of Man.

The beings of thought are given the name "little one" further along in The Tripartite Tractate, perhaps suggesting that they sound like children in the ears of Jesus. The voices themselves, however, are only dimly aware that it is Jesus to whom they are speaking.

"Just as the beings of thought had been given the name 'little one,' so they have a faint notion that they have the exalted one—he exists before them—and they have sown within them an attitude of amazement at the exalted one who will become manifest. Therefore they welcomed his revelation and they worshipped him. They became convinced witnesses to him. They acknowledged the light which had come into being, as one stronger than those who fought against them."

Having realized who Jesus is, the childlike voices then worship him and bear witness about him, having become convinced of his divinity and authority.

There is also another entity assigned to the care of Jesus, "a fellow sufferer with him, gives him rest little by little, makes him grow, lifts him up, gives himself to him completely for enjoyment from a vision." This is again an extremely complex look into the actual working consciousness of Jesus. This same entity is described by saying, "It was light and was a desire to be established and an openness for instruction and an eye for vision, qualities which it had from the exalted ones. It was also wisdom for his thinking in opposition to the things beneath the organization. It was also a word for speaking and the perfection of things of this sort."

It seems that there is an entity living inside Jesus who instructs him in wisdom somehow through the medium of his eyes, through instructive visions. The entity also helps Jesus choose the words he is to speak, and helps him separate the wheat from the chaff as Jesus observes the world around him. The combination of childlike voices and the visual companion are called by the term "the organization." Is this a picture of the inner workings of the mind of Jesus? Is it the kind of glimpse into the mysteries of the Divine Son of God that mankind has sought for two millennia?

The thing is, it all seems perfectly logical, like it would be appropriate to the task of filling in the gaps of our knowledge of just how Jesus thought and felt and was capable of his many miracles—not just of the "changing water into wine" type, but also his miraculous leaps of logic and the profound use of language with which he revealed the Kingdom of Heaven to his followers and the world that came after. He obviously had some kind of help from heaven above, and The Tripartite Tractate might represent a complete and truthful revelation of just what that help was.

Chapter Twelve
The Gospel Of The Egyptians

- Do such strange images as a "four-breasted virgin" copulating with the savior figure called Seth and the transmission of his "seed" to a faraway star imply aspects of the alien breeding program?
- Read about the End Times as prophesied in The Gospel of the Egyptians. Do fire, famine and plagues await us?
- Did the heavenly spirit Seth occupy Jesus' body and wear him like a garment? What was the real source of Jesus' holiness?

The Gospel of the Egyptians, sometimes alternately called The Holy Book of the Great Invisible Spirit, contains many diverse and interesting elements, including some End Times prophecy and a quite different theory of Christ, namely that he was in fact the great spirit Seth, analogous to the third Son of Adam, who had put on the appearance of Christ as a garment.

THE ALIEN WHO CREATED HIMSELF

The book begins with a long section of creation myth in which the Father is first established as, "the great invisible Spirit, the Father whose name cannot be uttered, he who came forth from the heights of the perfection, the light of the light of the heavenly powers of light, the light of the silence and the Father of the silence, the light of the word and the truth, the light of the incorruptions, the infinite light, the radiance from the powers of light of the unrevealable, unmarked, ageless, unproclaimable Father, the power of the powers, self-begotten, self-producing, alien, the really true power."

(The phrase "self-begotten, self-producing, alien," is taken verbatim from the text, by the way. If one were prone to say that the real truth is in the details, one might wonder at the insertion of "alien" into the description of the Father, but that may have to await a later date for further inspection.)

The Father then brings forth from himself the entities called "Mother" and "Son," followed by a further begetting of various beings given obscure spiritual names. The text is hard to follow at that point, but concerns the establishment of heavenly structure and the division of power among the many spiritual domains given life by the Father's creative prowess. In a moment reminiscent of Genesis, when God looks upon his creation and adjudges it to be good, in the Gospel of the Egyptians it says, "And the Father nodded approval."

A short time later, "Then everything shook, and trembling took hold of the incorruptible ones. Then the three male children came forth from above, down into the unborn ones, and the self-begotten ones, and those who were begotten in what is begotten. The greatness came forth, the whole greatness of the great Christ. He established thrones in glory, myriads without number, powers and glories and incorruptions."

Christ in the role of creator then produces "the incorruptible, spiritual church," and "the god of truth, praising, singing, and giving glory with one voice, with one accord, and a mouth which does not rest, to the Father, the Mother and the Son, and the fullness of their deity."

A DOSE OF HIGH STRANGENESS KICKS IN

It at this point that we are told that the great Seth, the son of the incorruptible Adamas, "gave praise to the great, invisible, uncallable, unnameable, virginal Spirit, and the male virgin and the thrice male child . . . . Then there came forth from that place the great power of the great light, the mother of the angels, the mother of the lights, the glorious mother, the virgin with the four breasts, bringing the fruit from Gomorrah as spring, and Sodom, which is the fruit of the spring of Gomorrah which is in her. She came forth through the great Seth."

What are we to make of a "four-breasted virgin" and the apparent portrayal of Sodom and Gomorrah as locations as pure as the spring air? Not your usual Biblical fare, is it?

Seth then has some form of intercourse with the four-breasted virgin and takes his "seed" to a place called "Davithe," the "third great light." Perhaps that last is a description of a faraway star? Are we perhaps reading yet another account of alien breeding experiments here? Something similar to the familiar passage from Genesis Six in which the Sons of God come down and take as wives the daughters of men? Some of the imagery seems similar, though the children created this time are not left on earth to create havoc and wickedness but are transported to what may be the great Seth's home planet.

"After five thousand years," the Gospel of the Egyptians continues, "the great light Eleleth spoke: 'Let someone rule over the chaos and Hades.' And there appeared a cloud whose name is Sophia. She looked out on the parts of chaos, her face being like blood."

The statement about finding someone to rule over chaos and Hades is repeated by the angel Gamaliel, after which the cloud Sophia becomes agreeable to the idea.

"Then Sakla, the great angel, saw the great demon who is with him, Nebruel. And they became together a begetting spirit of the earth. They begot assisting angels."

From a four-breasted virgin we have moved on to an angel copulating with a demon and producing twelve angels. But after that moment in creation is finished, the angel Sakla said to his angels, "I, I am a jealous god, and apart from me nothing has come into being."

"Then a voice came from on high, saying, 'The man exists, and the Son of Man.'"

The drama then returns to the story of Seth.

"Then the great angel Hormos came to prepare, through the virgins of the corrupted sowing of this power, in a Logos-begotten, holy vessel, through the holy Spirit, the seed of the great Seth. Then the great Seth came and brought his seed. It was sown in the powers of heaven, which had been brought forth, their number being the amount of Sodom. Some say that Sodom is the place of pasture of the great Seth, which is Gomorrah. But others say that the great Seth took his plant out of Gomorrah and planted it in the second place to which he gave the name Sodom."

And once again we hear of Sodom and Gomorrah as blessed locations, not the vile cities of wickedness and sin so familiar from the Book of Genesis. It is all a bit confusing, to say the least.

THE TIME OF THE END

The Gospel of the Egyptians then shifts into a little end time prophesying.

"This is the race which came forth through Edokla. For she gave birth through the word to Truth and Justice, the origin of the seed of the eternal life which is with those who will persevere because of the knowledge of their emanation. This is the great, incorruptible race, which has come forth through three worlds to the world.

"And the flood came as an example for the consummation of the heavenly powers. But it will be sent into the world because of this race. A conflagration will come upon the earth. And grace will be with those who belong to the race through the prophets and the guardians who guard the life of the race. Because of this race, famines will occur, and plagues. But these things will happen because of the great incorruptible race. Because of this race, temptations will come, a falsehood of false prophets."

You just said a mouthful. This one chunk of scripture contains so much already familiar from the New Testament. The idea of the earth being destroyed by fire, the "conflagration" the passage mentions, is accompanied by a prediction of famines and plagues, and a plentitude of false and deceiving prophets. But through it all will endure the "incorruptible race," the pure and the chosen and the righteous, who are in part responsible for the various tribulations, which are sent perhaps to test and prove the enduring worth of the righteous.

"Then the great Seth saw the activity of the devil, and his many guises, and his schemes which will come upon his incorruptible, immovable race, and the persecutions of his powers and his angels and their error, that they acted against themselves."

As in the Book of Revelation, the devil has a role to play in making war against the righteous, with his demons alongside him, but the devil's strategies will ultimately prove self-defeating.

THE NATURE OF JESUS

A vast host of angels is sent to guard over the chosen race. Meanwhile, Seth has passed through three different phases of the apocalypse: the flood, the conflagration and the final judgment. He prepares a new body for himself.

"A Logos-begotten body which the great Seth prepared for himself, secretly through the virgin, in order that the saints may be begotten by the Holy Spirit, through invisible, secret symbols, through a reconciliation of the world with the world, through the renouncing of the world, through the convocation of the saints and the ineffable ones, and the incorruptible bosom, and through the great light of the Father, who preexisted with his Providence and established her through her holy baptism that surpasses the heaven, through the incorruptible, Logos-begotten one, even Jesus the living one, he whom the great Seth has put on."

This new body Seth has prepared is the physical container of Seth's spirit called Jesus, born secretly through a virgin, that he might reconcile "the world with the world." That last is a wonderfully evocative phrase, reminiscent of Robert Frost's masterful "A lover's quarrel with the world."

Seth offers a prayer to the one who has created him.

"This great name of thine is upon me, O self-begotten Perfect One, who art not outside me. I see thee, O thou who art visible to everyone. For who will be able to comprehend thee in another tongue? Now that I have known thee, I have mixed myself with the immutable. I have armed myself with an armor of light; I have become light. For the Mother was at that place because of the splendid beauty of grace.

"Therefore I have stretched out my hands while they were folded. I was shaped in the circle of the riches of the light, which is in my bosom, which gives shape to the many begotten ones in the light into which no complaint reaches. I shall declare thy glory truly, for I have comprehended thee, O God of silence! I honor thee completely.

"Thou art my place of rest, O Son, the formless one who exists in the formless ones, who exists, raising up the man in whom thou wilt purify me into thy life, according to thine imperishable name. Therefore the incense of life is in me. I mixed it with water, after the model of all the heavenly powers, in order that I might live with thee in the peace of the saints, thou who exists really truly forever."

THE BOOK IS HIDDEN AWAY

Having spoken his very moving prayer, Seth next conceals the book in order that it may be revealed later.

"This is the book which the great Seth wrote," The Gospel of the Egyptians says, "and placed in high mountains on which the sun has not risen, nor is it possible. And since the days of the prophets, and the apostles, and the preachers, the name has not at all risen upon their hearts, nor is it possible. And their ear has not heard it.

"The great Seth wrote this book with letters in one hundred and thirty years. He placed it in the mountain that is called Charaxio, in order that, at the end of the times and the eras, by the will of the divine, fullness of God, through the gift of the untraceable, unthinkable fatherly love, it may come forth and reveal this incorruptible, holy race of the great savior, and those who dwell with them in love, and the great, invisible eternal Spirit, and his only begotten Son, and the eternal light, and his great, incorruptible consort, and the incorruptible Wisdom, and the fullness of God in eternity."

Was Seth somehow able to anticipate the fact that his book would be buried away and not recovered until the Nag Hammadi find of 1945? Are we living in that era he called "the end of the times?" And has all of human history been directed toward the fulfillment of what Seth calls "the incorruptible, holy race of the great savior"? While those questions must obviously remain unanswered here, The Gospel of the Egyptians provides much food for thought for believers in prophecy and those who share in the hope that "the meek will inherit the earth."

Chapter Thirteen
A Different Version Of The Eden Story

- Was the God who cast Adam and Eve out of paradise a blind and arrogant sinner himself?
- What was the serpent's true role in tempting Adam and Eve to eat the forbidden fruit? Could the serpent have been in reality a wise teacher?
- If Yahweh the Creator is evil, then who is there to rescue us from him? Is there a higher God we can call on?

As mentioned earlier in this book, the Gnostics often took a very different approach to the story of Adam and Eve in the Garden of Eden as told in Genesis. One prominent example of this "heretical" view is told in a book from the Nag Hammadi collection called The Hypostasis Of The Archons, which translates more simply as The Reality Of The Rulers.

Scholars have determined that this book includes both Jewish and Christian elements, as well as acknowledging the authority of the Apostle Paul, in what is basically a work of mythology that points the finger of blame for mankind's hardships on the blind creator called God in the traditional Genesis.

The book begins by quoting St. Paul as saying, "Our contest is not against flesh and blood, but rather the authorities of the universe and the spirits of wickedness."

YAHWEH IS MISTAKEN

Next, the God who says, "It is I who am God; there is none apart from me," is said to have sinned against "the entirety." A voice from above, from "incorruptibility," quickly answers him by saying, "You are mistaken, Samael," meaning "god of the blind."

The thoughts of the vain "god" become blinder still, and he pursues his blasphemy down to chaos and the abyss. Meanwhile, back on earth, "the rulers" of the book's title say to one another, "Come, let us create a man that will be soil from the earth."

They proceed to create such a man, modeled after their own image and after a vision of God they had beheld at some time previous. But not understanding the force of God, because of their powerlessness, they are unable to bring the man to life. God comes and breathes on the face of the man, which gives the man a soul. But still they cannot get the new creation to arise and walk. They continue to blow on him incessantly, but they cannot summon the power to make him live.

Eventually, a spirit sees the "soul-endowed man" and comes down to dwell inside him, which finally makes the man a living creature. He is given the name Adam and the rulers supervising his life gather together all the animals and birds of the earth to see what names Adam will give them. Then they set Adam down in the midst of the garden for him to cultivate it. They also issue the familiar warning about not eating from the tree "of recognizing good and evil," or "with death you are going to die." At this point, the book declares that the rulers themselves don't understand the warning they've just given to Adam, for in so saying they have in fact forced him to eat from the tree. But that is for later.

SHE'S ALIVE!

The next step in the mythological story told here is the creation of woman.

"The rulers took counsel with one another and said, 'Come let us cause a deep sleep to fall upon Adam.' And he slept. Now the deep sleep that they caused to fall upon him, and he 'slept,' is Ignorance. They opened his side like a living woman. And they built up his side with some flesh in place of her, and Adam came to be endowed only with soul."

In other words, back to square one for Adam. The woman, who is now equipped with the spirit taken from Adam, comes to him and speaks to him, telling him to "arise." Adam then credits the female spirit with giving him true life, and calls her the "Mother of the living."

"For it is she who is my mother," Adam says. "It is she who is the physician, and the woman, and she who has given birth."

The reader understands at this point some of the Gnostic variations from the traditional Genesis story. Adam is created after a very tricky process of trial and error, and only when seen by a decidedly female deity does he in fact come to life for real. Our traditional image of a glowering Yahweh overseeing the process is totally contradicted here.

Then the authorities ruling over Adam find him speaking to his female counterpart and become greatly agitated. They also become greatly enamored of her and try to "sow their seed" inside her, giving chase for that purpose.

"And she laughed at them for their witlessness," the book continues, "and their blindness." She transforms herself into a tree, leaving only a shadowy reflection of herself behind her. The rulers pursuing her then begin to defile the tree! This again is quite a different story of the God ruling over Eden and how he interacts with his creations.

THE SERPENT TEACHER

"Then the female spiritual principle came in the snake, the instructor; and it taught them, saying, 'What did he say to you? Was it, "From every tree in the garden shall you eat; yet-from the tree of recognizing evil and good, do not eat?"

"The carnal woman said, 'Not only did he say "Do not eat," but even "Do not touch it; for from the day you eat from it, with death you are going to die."

"And the snake, the instructor, said, 'With death you shall not die; for it was out of jealousy that he said this to you. Rather, your eyes shall open and you shall come to be like gods, recognizing evil and good.' And the female instructing principle was taken away from the snake, and she left it behind merely a thing of the earth."

Again, some rather dramatic variations from the older version of the story. The snake is seen as the benevolent "instructor" of Adam and Eve, helping to free them from the jealous God who would keep them in ignorance. The snake is seen not as the incarnation of Satan himself, but rather as a simple creature of the earth momentarily taken over by the benevolent female spirit who speaks through it.

In any case, both Adam and Eve do indeed eat from the forbidden tree.

"And their imperfection became apparent in their lack of acquaintance; and they recognized that they were naked of the spiritual element, and took fig leaves and bound them upon their loins. Then the chief ruler came and he said, 'Adam! Where are you?' For he did not understand what had happened. And Adam said, 'I heard your voice and was afraid because I was naked; and I hid.' The ruler said, 'Why did you hide, unless it is because you have eaten from the tree from which alone I commanded you not to eat? And you have eaten!' Adam said, 'The woman that you gave me, she gave to me and I ate.' And the arrogant ruler cursed the woman."

Something very similar to this scene occurs in Genesis, though that account does not call God "the arrogant ruler" and imply that he is too blind to know where Adam is. The woman in her confession to God blames the snake, which was thereafter forever cursed, though it had played only an involuntary part in the drama while possessed by the female "instructor." This mistake is again put at the feet of this negative portrayal of the Yahweh god.

THE DAUGHTER OF ADAM AND EVE

The rulers of Eden then expel Adam and his woman from the garden, and forces them to toil continually and be occupied by worldly affairs, so that they have no opportunity to be devoted to the Holy Spirit. The births of Cain, Abel and Seth quickly follow, as well as Abel's death at the hands of his elder brother. Then comes the birth of a daughter named "Norea." Eve notes the moment by saying, "He has begotten on me a virgin as an assistance for many generations of mankind."

Norea is the virgin who is left undefiled by the powers-that-be.

"Then mankind began to multiply and improve. The rulers took counsel with one another and said, 'Come, let us cause a deluge with our hands and obliterate all flesh, from man to beast.'"

This is a variant on the opening of the story of Noah and the ark, except that here the rulers have no desire to punish mankind's wickedness, but rather to put a stop to how he has multiplied and improved. An opposing ruler learns of the plot and tells Noah to make himself an ark with the requisite children and beasts and birds, which Noah obediently does. Norea, the virgin daughter mentioned above, comes to Noah and asks to be allowed to board the ark. When Noah refuses, she "blew upon the ark and caused it be consumed by fire. Again he made the ark, for a second time."

Meanwhile, the rulers went to meet her, intending to lead her astray. Their supreme chief said to her, "Your mother Eve came to us."

"But Norea turned to them and said to them, 'It is you who are the rulers of the darkness; you are accursed. And you did not know my mother; instead it was your female counterpart that you knew. For I am not your descendant; rather it is from the world above that I am come.'"

The "arrogant ruler" says that Norea must neveretheless do their bidding. Norea then sends up a prayer in a loud voice to "the holy one, the God of the entirety," saying, "Rescue me from the rulers of unrighteousness and save me from their clutches-forthwith!"

A great angel hears her plea and comes down from the heavens, saying, "Why are you crying up to God? Why do you act so boldly towards the Holy Spirit?"

To which Norea replies, "Who are you?"

The rulers have somehow "withdrawn from her," and the rescuing angel tells her his name.

"It is I who am Eleleth, sagacity, the great angel who stands in the presence of the Holy Spirit. I have been sent to speak with you and save you from the grasp of the lawless. And I shall teach you about your root."

Next, the author of The Reality Of The Rulers speaks to his audience, "Now as for that angel, I cannot speak of his power; his appearance is like fine gold and his raiment is like snow. No, truly, my mouth cannot bear to speak of his power and the appearance of his face."

The focus of the dialogue shifts to a conversation between the angel and the book's author.

The angel informs the author that the rulers have no power over him, that as a proper disciple of gnosis, the author cannot be defiled; his "abode is in incorruptibility, where the virgin spirit dwells, who is superior to the authorities of chaos and to their universe."

The angel says further that, "A veil exists between the world above and the realms that are below; and shadow came into being beneath the veil; and that shadow became matter; and that shadow was projected apart. And what she had created became a product in the matter, like an aborted fetus. And it assumed a plastic form molded out of shadow, and became an arrogant beast resembling a lion."

The arrogant lion-like creature was androgynous, we are told, and when he saw a vast quantity of matter without limit, he declared himself to be God, apart from whom there was no other. We are next revisited by the same voices as at the beginning, who call down to the arrogant creature that he is quite simply blind.

 He is swiftly rewarded by being given charge of the seventh heaven, and he sits there on The creature challenges them to prove him wrong, and quickly the female embodiment of wisdom, Sophia, introduces light into matter, and "she pursued it down to the region of chaos." The arrogant leonine creature continues to declare himself alone to be God, and is again contradicted. This time around, he is cast into a world below the abyss by a fiery angel. The son of the arrogant creature, on seeing the fate of his father, repents and condemns his evil parentagea throne, with the life-giving force on his right hand. When his arrogant father sees him in his splendor, he becomes jealous.

"And this was the origin of envy. And envy engendered death . . ."

But all of this is the beneficent will of the father of the entirety, who has a purpose for everything. Then the angel tells his audience that they are not descended from this evil lot, but rather that they are "from the primeval Father, from above, out of the imperishable light," and thus are safe from the arrogant rulers and authorities. They are even blessed to the extent that they "exist deathless in the midst of dying mankind."

The book ends with the promise of the coming of a "true man," who will "teach them about everything, and anoint them with the unction of life eternal, given him from the un-dominated generation. Then they will be freed of blind thought, and they will trample underfoot death, which is of the authorities, and they will ascend into the limitless light. Then the authorities will relinquish their ages, and their angels will weep, and their demons will lament their death.

"Then all of the children of the light will be truly acquainted with the truth and their root, and the father of the entirety and the Holy Spirit. They will all say with a single voice, 'The Father's truth is just, and the son presides over the entirety.'"

The promise of "a true man," a messiah sent from a God who is far above the mere arrogant tinkering in our traditional Genesis story, is intended to serve as inspiration for the book's audience. It offers the hope that they as the chosen of light will outlast the arrogant rulers, who are in fact "all too real," as the title of the book declares. Yet how odd that the dark ones denounced here are the same entities we in the non-Gnostic world have thought of as the true God since Sunday school. The variations from that story presented in The Reality of the Rulers certainly do get one to think in some interesting new directions!

Chapter Fourteen
God As Gender Bender

- What are we to make of the notion that the true creator of the universe was female in nature, at least part of the time?

- Is a Trinity of Father, Mother and Son more sacred than the traditional orthodox Trinity?

- How did the Heavenly Mother create the universe? With whom did she copulate in the days of prehistory?

The next book to be looked at is given yet another very complicated title, The Trimorphic Protennoia, which translates more simply as The Three-Formed Divine First Thought. As with previous Gnostic books, it offers up a vision of God as female, but then morphs into a strange kind of Creator who bends the gender factor in some surprising ways. But that will come a little later.

This book is said to have been revised and given new Christian overtones liberally borrowed from the Gospel of John. It begins with the first person declarations of a female entity named Protennoia.

A FEMALE GOD OF THE UNIVERSE

"I am Protennoia, the Thought that dwells in the light. I am the movement that dwells in the All, she in whom the All takes its stand, the first-born among those who came to be, she who exists before the All. She dwells alone, since she is perfect. I am invisible within the Thought of the Invisible One. I am revealed in the immeasurable, ineffable things. I am incomprehensible, dwelling in the incomprehensible. I move in every creature. I am the life that dwells within every Power and every eternal movement, and in the invisible lights and Angels and Demons and in every material soul. I dwell in those who came to be. I move in everyone and I delve into them all. I walk uprightly, and those who sleep I awaken. And I am the sight of those who dwell in sleep."

After some similar statements that lay claim to her being the original and ultimate Creator, Protennoia next calls herself a "voice."

"I am a Voice speaking softly," she declares. "I exist from the first. I dwell within the Silence that surrounds everything."

Protennoia next describes her descent into the underworld, where she creates the physical world as we know it.

"I shone down upon the darkness," she says. "It is I who poured forth the water. It is I who am hidden within radiant waters. I am the one who gradually put forth the All by my Thought. It is I who am laden with the Voice. It is through me that Gnosis comes forth."

Here is an apparent similarity to the Gospel of John. Protennoia creates by thought and speech, as the male God of the Gospel of John created by his Word.

THE TRINITY FAMILY STYLE

"I am perception and knowledge, uttering a Voice by means of thought. I am the real Voice. I cry out in everyone. I am the Thought of the Father. I am joined with everyone by virtue of the Hidden Thought. And it is immeasurable, since it dwells in the Immeasurable One."

This section introduces the concept of the Father, and is followed quickly by a description of the Son.

"Then the Son who is perfect in every respect—that is the Word, who originated through that Voice, who proceeded from the height, who has within him the Name; who is a Light—he the Son revealed the everlasting things and all the unknowns were known. And those things difficult to interpret and secret, he revealed, and as for those who dwell in Silence with the First Thought, he preached to them."

At which point we are presented with an interesting variation on the Trinity of Father, Son and Holy Ghost.

"Now the Voice that originated from my Thought exists as three permanences: the Father, the Mother, the Son. Existing perceptibly as speech, the Voice has within it a Word endowed with every glory, and it has three masculinities, three powers, and three names."

Some real gender bending in this section. First the part of the Trinity normally identified as the male or gender neutral "Holy Spirit" is here feminized and called the Mother. Then in the very next sentence, the Mother figure is grouped as part of "three masculinities" that form this new family-style Trinity. The shifting of gender back and forth is a little confusing, to say the least. The voice of Protennoia next claims credit for creating Christ herself, saying she "anointed him as the glory of the Invisible Spirit with goodness."

YAHWEH AS A DEMON

A short time later, an evil spirit makes an appearance.

"There appeared the great Demon, who rules over the lowest part of the underworld, and Chaos. He has neither form nor perfection, but on the contrary possesses the form of the glory of those begotten in the darkness. Now he is called 'Saklas,' that is 'Samael,' 'Yaltabaoth,' he who has taken power; who had snatched it away from the innocent one (Sophia, or Wisdom); who had earlier overpowered her who is the Light."

This is the same blind, egomaniacal version of the God of the Bible mentioned in earlier chapters, the one traditional Christianity calls Yahweh and the Heavenly Father. In his role as the great Demon, he begins to create likenesses of genuine heavenly things. After some further give and take between him and the voice of Protennoia, she tells how she breaks the chains of the demons of the underworld and liberates the Sons of Light from imprisonment in the darkness.

Then, reiterating her essentially female nature, she says, "I am the Mother of the Voice, speaking in many ways, completing the All. It is in me that knowledge dwells, the knowledge of things everlasting. Now I have come the second time in the likeness of a female, and have spoken. And I shall tell them of the coming end of the Age and teach them of the beginning of the Age to come, the one without change, the one in which our appearances shall be changed."

Some interesting End Times prophesying there. A time is coming that will not change, but we ourselves will be changed to be made ready for it. This is typical of New Testament prophesying, as when the Apostle Paul says, "We shall all be changed" in the twinkling of an eye. It is also characterized as moment of birth, what Christ calls the time of "a woman in travail."

"The birth beckons: hour begets hour, day begets day. Just as the pangs of time had drawn near, so also had the destruction approached. All together the elements trembled, and the foundations of the underworld and the ceilings of Chaos shook and a great fire shone within their midst, and the rocks and the earth were shaken like a reed shaken by the wind."

The apocalyptic destruction also disturbs the powers-that-be.

"And the lots of Fate and those who apportion the domiciles were greatly disturbed over a great thunder. And the thrones of the Powers were disturbed, since they were overturned, and their King was afraid."

There is a general confusion about just what is ripping apart the status quo, after which the Voice then reveals herself to the Sons of Thought, saying, "Listen to me, to the Speech of the Mother of your mercy, for you have become worthy of the mystery hidden from the beginning of the Ages, so that you might receive it."

And what is this great mystery that they are now privileged to know?

"I am androgynous," Protennoia says. "I am Mother and I am Father, since I copulate with myself. I copulated with myself, and with those who love me, and it is through me alone that the All stands firm. I am the Womb that gives shape to the All by giving birth to the light that shines in splendor. I am the Age to come. I am the fulfillment of the All, that is, the glory of the Mother. I cast speech into the ears of those who hear me."

The book closes with a section in which Protennoia repeats her claims to be the ultimate creator of all things and again declares Christ to be another aspect of herself, saying, "I put on Jesus [as one would put on a garment]. I bore him from the cursed wood, and established him in the dwelling places of his Father. And those who watch over their dwelling places did not recognize me. For I, I am unrestrainable, together with my Seed, and my Seed, which is mine, I shall place into the Holy Light, within an incomprehensible Silence. Amen."

Even this closing paragraph contains some subtle gender-bending. Protennoia, as a female entity, describes placing her "seed" into the Holy Light. The word "seed," a traditional euphemism for "semen" or "sperm," is definitely on the male side of the equation, is it not?

So what are we to make of all the shifting of gender and sexual roles in this book? Whether it is possible or not to make a literal kind of sense of it, it is in any case a huge departure from the Biblical patriarchal/male-centered view of the world. It is often argued that one reason that the Virgin Mary is so important to some people's understanding of Christianity is because believers have a deeply imbedded need to see that the feminine principle of life is given some degree of dignity, that the womanly half of the world counts for something important alongside the bearded ancients who dominate the stories of the Bible.

In the case of the Trimorphic Protennoia, that same crying out for the feminine may underlie the book's author's decision to paint a portrait of the Creator God whose work under-girds all of reality not only as a woman, but also as an androgynous entity who essentially "copulates" with herself/himself—and with those who "love" her/him—to create the universe. Just another example of some of the strange twists on the traditional stories that were discovered at Nag Hammadi that fateful day in 1945.

Chapter Fifteen
The Laughing Jesus: Differing Versions Of The Crucifixion

- Read some historical accounts of the crucifixion of Jesus as recorded by the Romans and the Jewish historian Josephus. Their perception of what happened is quite different.

- Did Jesus somehow rise above his suffering on the cross? Did he, in a manner of speaking, die laughing?

- We have long been told that Jesus was a normal human being in most respects. But what if he was decidedly something else?

The crucifixion of Jesus Christ is perhaps the primary point on which all schools of Christianity agree. That Jesus suffered and died under Pontius Pilate has also been attested to by various non-Christian historians of the time.

THE VIEW FROM OUTSIDE THE FAITH

Elaine Pagels, in what has come to be regarded as a classic work of religious history, **The Gnostic Gospels**, makes reference to the Roman historian Tacitus, who knew virtually nothing about Jesus. But in his account of the infamous emperor Nero, Tacitus describes how Nero falsely put the blame on Christians for starting major fires in Rome, saying he "substituted as culprits and punished with the utmost refinements of cruelty a class of persons hated for their vices, whom the crowd called Christians.

Christus, the founder of the name, had undergone the death penalty in the reign of Tiberius, by sentence of the procurator Pontius Pilate, and the pernicious superstition was checked for a moment, only to break out once more, not only in Judea, the home of the disease, but in the capital itself, where everything horrible or shameful in the world gathers and becomes fashionable."

The reader, on first encountering this Roman-eye-view of Jesus and the crucifixion, may find it a little strange to see the familiar historical points from such a different perspective. If history is indeed written by the winners, it is obvious that the traditional Christian view long ago won that battle of truth.

The renowned Jewish historian Josephus mentions Jesus of Nazareth in a list of problems that beset Jewish relations with Rome when Pilate was governor. That list included this statement from Josephus: "Pilate, having heard him accused by men of the highest standing among us, condemned him to be crucified."

Of course, all this testimony from the so-called "objective historians" is borne out by the New Testament accounts of the crucifixion, with the difference being that they interpret the circumstances leading to Jesus' death as being the results of his innocence, not his spreading of an evil superstition as the Romans and Jews said.

LAUGHING THROUGH THE PAIN

But what do the Gnostics say about the crucifixion? According to Pagels, their interpretation differs greatly in many ways. For instance, one of the books found at Nag Hammadi, The Apocalypse of Peter, relates the following account.

"I saw him apparently being seized by them. And I said, 'What am I seeing, O Lord? Is it really you whom they take? And are you holding on to me? And are they hammering the feet and hands of another? Who is this one above the cross, who is glad and laughing?' The Savior said to me, 'He whom you saw being glad and laughing above the cross is the Living Jesus. But he into whose hands and feet they are driving the nails is his fleshly part, which is the substitute. They put to shame that which remained in his likeness. And look at him, and look at me.'"

Certainly this is an unusual portrayal of the crucifixion. The image of Christ looking down on his own suffering in a spirit of gladness and laughter could not be more different than the attitude of extreme suffering, even shameful nakedness, that is taught in the conventional telling of the story. Pagels moves on to quote from The Second Treatise of the Great Seth, an even stranger variation on the story.

"It was another who drank the gall and vinegar; it was not I. They struck me with the reed; it was another, Simon, who bore the cross on his shoulder. It was another upon whom they placed the crown of thorns. But I was rejoicing in the height over their error, and I was laughing at their ignorance."

A NON-HUMAN JESUS

Again with the laughter from a view above all the suffering. Just what is going on here? According to Pagels, passages like these were intended to show that Jesus was not completely human. Instead, he was a spiritual being who adapted himself to human perception. Pagels quotes from The Acts of John, referred to earlier in this book, in which James once saw Jesus standing on the shore in the form of a child, but when he pointed Jesus out to John, "I [John] said, 'Which child?' And he answered me, 'The one who is beckoning to us.' And I said, 'This is because of the long watch we have kept at sea. You are not seeing straight, brother James. Do you not see the man standing there who is handsome, fair and cheerful looking?' But he said to me, 'I do not see that man, my brother.'"

When the two go ashore, Jesus has changed his form once again, appearing to John as a baldheaded man with a thick flowing beard, but to his brother James as a young man only just beginning to grow a beard. Sometimes when John touches Jesus, he encounters solid flesh, but at other times Jesus' substance was "immaterial and incorporeal, as if it did not exist at all." Jesus leaves no footprints, and he never blinks his eyes.

"All of this demonstrates to John," Pagels writes, "that Jesus' nature was spiritual, not human."

Which of course allows for the Gnostic variations on whether Jesus actually suffered on the cross, or sent a substitute instead, while he himself floated high above the torture and laughed in a general attitude of gladness.

AND THEY DANCED

According to Pagel and the Gnostics, Jesus was also quite the dancer.

"The Acts of John goes on to tell how Jesus, anticipating arrest, joined with his disciples in Gethsemane the night before:

"He assembled us all, and said, 'Before I am delivered to them, let us sing a hymn to the Father, and so go to meet what lies before us.' So he told them to form a circle, holding one another's hands, and himself stood in the middle . . ."

Jesus then begins to lead the disciples in a mystical chant, which reads, in part,

"To the Universe belongs the dancer,

"He who does not dance does not know what happens

"Now if you follow my dance, see yourself in Me who am speaking

"You who dance, consider what I do, for yours is this passion of Man which I am about to suffer, For you could by no means have understood what you suffer, unless to you as the Word I had been sent by the Father,

"Learn how to suffer and you shall not be able to suffer."

THE EXCLUDED BOOKS OF THE BIBLE - UPDATED

The story told by John continues, "After the Lord had danced with us, my beloved, he went out to suffer. And we were like men amazed or fast asleep, and we fled this way and that."

Later, Jesus appears in a vision to John, saying that the crucifixion happening at that moment is a delusion and not something real.

"I have suffered none of the things which they will say of me," Jesus tells John. "Even that suffering which I showed to you and to the rest in my dance, I will that it be called a mystery."

That mystery includes the idea that since Jesus was the Son of Man, being human, he suffered and died like the rest of humanity. But as the Son of God, the divine spirit within him could not die, and so he transcended suffering and death.

"Yet orthodox Christians," Pagels writes, "insist that Jesus was a human being, and that all 'straight-thinking' Christians must take the crucifixion as a historical and literal event. Pope Leo the Great condemned such writings as the Acts of John as a 'hotbed of manifold perversity' which 'should not only be forbidden, but entirely destroyed and burned with fire.'"

What are we to make today of this vision of the laughing Jesus, one whose crucifixion may have been suffered by a surrogate victim? Or of a Jesus leading the disciples in a kind of universal dance of death, as though his coming suffering was to be celebrated with a joyful step out on to the dance floor? The sheer strangeness of the Gnostic vision of Jesus at the very least keeps us interested, does it not?

Chapter Sixteen
The Soul As A Suffering Whore

- Read about one of the strangest metaphors in the history or religion. Has the soul of humankind prostituted itself in the public streets?

- Can there be sexual intercourse on the soul level? Is sex more satisfying in that plane of existence?

- What form must repentance take so that the "soul-as-whore" can be saved?

The title for this chapter may sound strange, even blasphemous, but it is in fact the story told by the Gnostic book called *The Exegesis On The Soul*. The soul is designated as a female entity, and in no uncertain terms.

"Wise men of old gave the soul a feminine name," the book begins. "Indeed, she is female in her nature as well. She even has a womb."

THE FALL FROM GRACE

The soul begins her existence alone with the heavenly father. She is both a virgin and androgynous.

"But when she fell down into a body," the story continues, "and came to this life, then she fell into the hands of many robbers. And the wanton creatures passed her from one to another. Some made use of her by force, while others did so by seducing her with a gift.

"And in her body she prostituted herself, and gave herself to one and all, considering each one she was about to embrace to be her husband. When she had given herself to wanton, unfaithful adulterers, so that they might make use of her, then she sighed deeply and repented."

But the soul still cannot escape her fate.

"But even when she turns her face from those adulterers, she runs to others and they compel her to live with them and render service to them upon their bed, as if they were her masters. Out of shame, she no longer dares to leave them, whereas they deceive her for a long time, pretending to be faithful, true husbands, as if they greatly respected her. And after all this, they abandon her and let her go."

The soul sinks into poverty and widowhood, without even anything to eat. She has gained nothing from the sinful men she lay with but defilement and impurity. Her children by the adulterers are dumb, blind and sickly, even feebleminded.

It is then that the soul repents again and is heard by the Father.

"But when the father who is above visits her, and looks down upon her, and sees her sighing—with her sufferings and disgrace—and repenting of the prostitution in which she engaged, and when she begins to call on his name, so that he might help her, saying, 'Save me, my father, for behold I will render an account to thee, for I abandoned my house and fled from my maiden's quarters. Restore me to thyself again.' When he sees her in such a state, then he will count her worthy of his mercy upon her, for many are the afflictions that have come upon her because she abandoned her house."

WHORES DOWN THROUGH THE AGES

The writer of *The Exegesis On The Soul* then begins to quote verses from familiar scripture, starting with the Book of Jeremiah. Part of the quotation reads, "Take an honest look and see where you prostituted yourself. Were you not sitting in the streets, defiling the land with your acts of prostitution and your vices? You became shameless with everyone. You did not call on me as kinsman or as father or author of your virginity."

The Gnostic author then quotes another Old Testament prophet, Hosea, saying in part, "I shall remove her prostitution from my presence, and I shall remove her adultery from between her breasts. I shall make her naked as on the day she was born, and I shall make her desolate like a land without water, and I shall make her longingly childless. I shall show her children no pity, for they are children of prostitution, since their mother prostituted herself and put her children to shame."

The denunciation of prostitution gets even more brutally frank in a quote from Ezekiel.

"It came to pass, after much depravity, said the Lord, that you built yourself a brothel, and you made yourself a beautiful place in the streets. And you built yourself brothels on every lane, and you wasted your beauty and you spread your legs in every alley, and you multiplied your acts of prostitution. You prostituted yourself to the sons of Egypt, those who are your neighbors, men great of flesh."

"Yet the greatest struggle has to do with prostitution of the soul," the author of Exegesis On The Soul writes, as he segues from Old Testament quotes to quotes from First Corinthians and Ephesians.

"For our struggle is not against flesh and blood," according to the Apostle Paul, "but against the world rulers of darkness and the spirits of wickedness."

Then the author shifts back to the narrative of the wayward soul again.

"As long as the soul keeps running about everywhere copulating with whomever she meets and defiling herself, she exists suffering her just desserts. But when she perceives the straits she is in, and weeps before the father and repents, then the father will have mercy on her and he will make her womb turn from the external domain and will turn it again inward, so that the soul will regain her proper character. For it is not so with a woman. For the womb of the body is inside the body like the other internal organs, but the womb of the soul is around the outside, like the male genitalia, which are external."

The physical transformation being described here is a little hard to understand. Just what is an "outer womb," and how is it similar to the male genitalia? This kind of gender bending also occurs elsewhere in the Gnostic scriptures, and is a marked departure from the strictly defined standards of male and female found in the traditional books of the Bible.

The transformation is also referred to as a cleansing process that allows the soul to return to its former state of innocence. Then strangely enough, the soul begins to rage at itself, like a woman in labor, "who writhes and rages in the hour of delivery."

THE INTERCOURSE OF THE SOUL

But being a simple female, she cannot produce offspring on her own, so the Heavenly Father sends her a man who is her brother, the firstborn, who is also to be her bridegroom. The soul has given up her former prostitution and cleansed herself, so she is now renewed and fit to be married. She begins to fill the bridal chamber with perfume as she awaits the coming of the bridegroom. Like many an expectant wife, she waits to see what he will look like and when he will arrive.

The bridegroom arrives and sets about decorating the bridal chamber. The couple then has a chaste form of intercourse together.

"For since that marriage is not like the carnal marriage, those who are to have intercourse with one another will be satisfied with that intercourse. And, as if it were a burden, they leave behind them the annoyance of physical desire and they turn their faces from each other. But once they unite with one another, they become a single life."

This is said to be in keeping with Genesis 2:24, "They will become a single flesh."

"For the master of the woman is her husband," the Exegesis continues. "Then gradually she recognized him, and she rejoiced once more, weeping before him as she remembered the disgrace of her former widowhood. And she adorned herself still more so that he might be pleased with her."

We are next told that the soul is now required to turn her face from the multitude of adulterers and to turn her face to her king, her real lord, and to forget the earthly father, with whom things went badly for her.

The subject of intercourse with her new bridegroom is again broached, this time producing good children, which the soul begins to raise.

"For this is the great, perfect marvel of birth. And so this marriage is made perfect by the will of the father."

Which brings us to the next stage. The soul is now to return to her former state, as a child of God in heaven.

"Now it is fitting that the soul regenerate herself and become again as she formerly was. The soul then moves of her own accord. And she received the divine nature from the father for her rejuvenation, so that she might be restored to the place where originally she had been. This is the resurrection that is from the dead. This is the ransom from captivity. This is the upward journey of ascent into heaven. This is the way of ascent to the father."

The soul's youth is restored, and the author says that this represents the state of being "born again" familiar to us from the Gospels.

"Thus it is by being born again that the soul will be saved."

REPENTING OF THE WORLD

But we are cautioned that our repentance must be deep and heartfelt and not the empty rote words of the insincere.

"Repenting for the life we lived, confessing our sins, perceiving the empty deception we were in, and the empty zeal, weeping over how we were in darkness and in the wave, mourning for ourselves that he might have pity on us, hating ourselves for how we are now."

The author then quotes further passages from both the Old and New Testament about repentance and forgiveness. Then, oddly enough, the author moves on to quote from Homer's *The Odyssey,* saying first that, "Indeed, it is in order that he might know who is worthy of salvation that God examines the inward parts and searches the bottom of the heart. For no one is worthy of salvation who still loves the place of deception. Therefore it is written in the poet Homer, 'Odysseus sat on the island weeping and grieving and turning his face from the words of Calypso, and from her tricks, longing to see his village and smoke coming forth from it. And had he not received help from heaven, he would not have been able to return to his village.'"

The author of *The Exegesis On The Soul* interestingly includes some extra-Biblical sources here, but the same idea of breaking free of the delusional pleasures of the world to attain a state of repentance is repeated. The evidence of Greek influences on the author makes for a more broadminded approach, something akin to our own "comparative mythology."

All's well that ends well, right? *The Exegesis On The Soul* concludes by saying, "If we repent, truly God will heed us, he who is longsuffering and abundantly merciful, to whom is the glory forever and ever. Amen."

Chapter Seventeen
Did Jesus Have A Twin Brother?

- The Bible records that Jesus had several brothers and sisters, but it is only the Gnostics who refer to a twin named Judas Thomas. Read an account of a conversation between the two.
- Does being born through sexual intercourse make us akin to the lower animals? And does lust ensnare us in a world of illusion?
- Is hell full of madness and crazy laughter? Are the damned too dense to know where they really are?

The Book of Thomas the Contender from the Nag Hammadi find is written in a literary form called a "revelation dialogue," in this case a conversation between Jesus and his twin brother Judas Thomas. The book is mostly taken up with denunciations of the lustful and the wicked, against which the good person must struggle, hence the Contender part of the title.

The conversation is said to have been copied down by someone named Mathaias, who walks alongside the two brothers as Jesus and Thomas conduct their dialogue. The book begins with Jesus acknowledging his kinship to Thomas.

"The savior said, 'Brother Thomas, while you have time in the world, listen to me, and I will reveal to you the things you have pondered in your mind. Now since it has been said that you are my twin and true companion, examine yourself and learn who you are, in what way you exist, and how you will come to be. Since you will be called my brother, it is not fitting that you be ignorant of yourself. So while you accompany me, although you are uncomprehending, you have in fact already come to know, and you will be called "one who knows himself."

Then Jesus speaks one of the most basic doctrines of Gnosticism, that self-knowledge is knowledge of the divine.

"For he who has not known himself has known nothing, but he who has known himself has at the same time already achieved knowledge about the depth of all. So then, you, my brother Thomas, have beheld what is obscure to men, that is, what they ignorantly stumble against."

The dialogue between Jesus and Thomas is taking place after the resurrection but before the ascension. So Thomas appropriately says, "Therefore I beg you to tell me what I ask you before your ascension, and when I hear from you about the hidden things, then I can speak about them. And it is obvious to me that the truth is difficult to perform before men."

Jesus begins to talk about the visible things of the material world, explaining that lusts of the flesh are a consuming hell fire. The visible things lead ultimately to corruption.

BIRTH IS BEASTLY

"But these visible bodies," Jesus says, "survive by devouring creatures similar to them, with the result that the bodies change. Now that which changes will decay and perish, and has no hope of life from then on, since that body is bestial. So just as the body of the beasts perishes, so also will these formations perish. Do they not derive from intercourse, like that of the beasts? If the body too derives from intercourse, how will it beget anything different from the beasts? So, therefore, you are babes until you become perfect."

Here Jesus decries even the individual soul's birth into this world, because it is created by an act of intercourse, like those creatures of the animal kingdom. The doctrine of original sin from Genesis and some of the bleak outlook of the Book of Ecclesiastes are echoed here.

Thomas responds by saying that while this teaching is true, it will be difficult to go forth and preach about it.

"Therefore I say to you, lord, that those who speak about things that are invisible and difficult to explain are like those who shoot their arrows at a target at night. To be sure, they shoot their arrows as anyone would—since they shoot at the target—but it is not visible. Yet when the light comes forth and hides the darkness, then the work of each will appear. And you, your light, enlighten O Lord."

Jesus then launches into another attack on the lusts of the flesh.

"O unsearchable love of the light! O bitterness of the fire that blazes in the bodies of men and in their marrow, kindling in them night and day, and burning the limbs of men, and making their minds become drunk and their souls become deranged. For the males move upon the females, and the females upon the males. Therefore it is said, 'Everyone who seeks the truth from true wisdom will make himself wings so as to fly, fleeing the lust that scorches the spirits of men.' And he will make himself wings to flee from every visible spirit."

LUST IS A DECEIVER

Further along in **The Book of Thomas the Contender**, Jesus continues his exhortations against lust.

"For that which guides [the lustful], the fire, will give them an illusion of truth, and will shine on them with a perishable beauty, and it will imprison them in a dark sweetness and captivate them with fragrant pleasure. And it will blind them with insatiable lust, and burn their souls, and become for them like a stake stuck in their heart, which they can never dislodge. And like a bit in the mouth it leads them according to its own desire.

"And it has chained them with its chains and bound all their limbs with the bitterness of bondage of lust for those visible things that will decay and change and swerve by impulse. They have always been attracted downwards; as they are killed, they are assimilated to all the beasts of the perishable realm."

Jesus also provides a spooky description of the fate of all those who are seduced by the visible.

"Only a little while longer," he says, "and that which is visible will dissolve; then shapeless shades will emerge and in the midst of tombs they will forever dwell upon the corpses in pain and corruption of soul."

Like a scene from a horror movie. The falsely beautiful things of the flesh dissolve and morph into a tortured cemetery where the condemned souls float above their corpses, awaiting further judgment.

Thomas again presses the question of how he is expected to preach all this after Jesus has ascended into heaven.

"What have we to say in the face of these things?" Thomas asks. "What shall we say to blind men? What doctrine should we express to these miserable mortals who say, 'We came to do good and not to curse,' and yet claim, 'Had we not been begotten in mortal flesh, we would not have known iniquity?'"

THE FIRES OF LUST AND HELL

Jesus replies with more of the same.

"Truly, as for those, do not esteem them as men, but regard them as beasts, for just as beasts devour one another, so also men of this sort devour one another. On the contrary, they are deprived of the Kingdom of Heaven since they love the sweetness of the fire and are servants of death who rush to corruption. They fulfill the lust of their fathers. They will be thrown down to the abyss, and be afflicted by the torment of the bitterness of their evil nature. Their mind is directed to their own selves, for their thought is occupied with their deeds. But it is the fire that will burn them."

This last involves an interesting use of metaphor. The sweet fire of lust that lures the wicked becomes transformed into the fires of hell, where the lost souls are made to contemplate their deeds on earth even as they burn in eternity.

Jesus also warns of what will happen to those who hear the future teachings of Thomas and do not regard them.

"Truly I tell you that he who will listen to your word and turn away his face or sneer at it or smirk at these things, truly I tell you that he will be handed over to the ruler above who rules over all the powers as their king, and he will turn that one around and cast him from heaven down to the abyss, and he will be imprisoned in a narrow dark place."

The fires of hell become inescapable.

"If [the lustful sinner] flees westward, he finds the fire. If he turns southward, he finds it there as well. If he turns northward, the threat of seething fire meets him again. Nor does he find the way to the east, so as to flee there and be saved, for he did not find it in the day that he was in the body, so that he might find it in the Day of Judgment."

POETRY FOR THE DAMNED

There begins a section where the term "woe" is repeated, a kind of lyrical listing of the terrors ahead for the lustful.

"Woe to you, godless ones," Jesus says, "who have no hope, who rely on things that will not happen.

"Woe to you who hope in the flesh and in the prison that will perish. How long will you be oblivious? Your hope is set upon the world, and your god is this life.

"Woe to you within the fire that burns in you, for it is insatiable.

"Woe to you because of the wheel that turns in your minds.

"Woe to you within the grip of burning that is in you, for it will devour your flesh openly and rend your souls secretly, and prepare you for your companions."

That last is sort of reminiscent of the old joke about going to hell. At least you won't feel lonely because all your friends will be there with you.

"Woe to you, captives, for you are bound in caverns. You laugh! In mad laughter you rejoice! You neither realize your perdition, nor do you reflect on your circumstances, nor have you understood that you dwell in darkness and death. On the contrary, you are drunk with the fire and full of bitterness. Your mind is deranged on account of the burning that is in you, and sweet to you are the poison and the blows of your enemies. And the darkness rose for you like the light, for you surrendered your freedom for servitude. You darkened your hearts and surrendered your thoughts to folly, and you filled your thoughts with the smoke of the fire that is in you. You baptized your souls in the water of darkness. You walked by your own whims."

Again, a very interesting decrying of the ways of the wicked. Their laughter is crazy, and they are too dense to realize they are already in hell. The metaphor of fire continues and the idea of pursuing one's sins as being a kind of prison is repeated.

There is still more on the subject of lust.

"Woe to you who love intimacy with womankind, and polluted intercourse with them.

"Woe to you in the grip of the powers of your body, for they will afflict you.

"Woe to you in the grip of the forces of the evil demons.

"Woe to you who beguile your limbs with fire. Who is it that will rain a refreshing dew on you to extinguish the mass of fire from you along with your burning? Who is it that will cause the sun to shine upon you to disperse the darkness in you and hide the darkness and polluted water?"

Intercourse with women is here called "polluted," and a thing ruled over by "evil demons." This approach to sexuality is often referred to as "asceticism," meaning the practice of denial and an overcoming of things of the body, such as lust and hunger for rich food, or other indulgences. It stands in marked contrast to the other Gnostic books that say for instance that Jesus would kiss Mary Magdalene on the mouth from time to time. Jesus himself says in the gospels that he came "eating and drinking" and was thus called a glutton and a drunkard. Just where does one draw the line when it comes to indulging one's self in the pleasures of the world? Apparently that is a function of just who you're listening to at a given moment, since the scriptures concerning Jesus are so self-contradictory on this point.

The Book of Thomas the Contender then switches from woes to blessings, and ends on a fairly upbeat note.

"Blessed are you," Jesus says, "who have prior knowledge of the stumbling blocks and who flee alien things.

"Blessed are you who are reviled and not esteemed on account of the love their lord has for them.

"Blessed are you who weep and are oppressed by those without hope, for you will be released from every bondage."

And there is this final warning: "Watch and pray that you not come to be in the flesh, but rather that you come forth from the bondage of the bitterness of this life. And as you pray, you will find rest, for you have left behind the suffering and disgrace. For when you come forth from the sufferings and the passions of the body, you will receive rest from the good one, and you will reign with the king."

The overarching point of all this is that the way to true happiness is through abstention from the things of the body. One trades the illusory pleasures of this world and the temporary happiness they bring for something much stronger, much more wise, that will bring about the true happiness of the soul who attains salvation. It is a familiar formula for contentment, but it is rarely so concretely expressed as here in The Book of Thomas the Contender.

Chapter Eighteen
Excluded Books Of Another Kind:
Jubilees, Jasher and Enoch

- The Apocryphal Books of the Bible, excluded from the canon for many centuries, contain alternate versions of familiar stories from the Bible. Read for instance how Satan is often added to the stories, making for some fascinating complications.

- There are miracles attributed to angels in the Book of Jasher that seem much like the holographic projections of today. Are illusions on the battlefield the stuff of God?

- Did the prophet Enoch undergo a typical alien abduction experience? Did he view paradise from a UFO?

   While the importance of the discovery at Nag Hammadi cannot be over-estimated, one should also not discount some of the other "lost" books of the Bible, often called the Apocrypha. For Biblical scholars, both professional and amateur, there has always been a keen fascination for the numerous ancient writings that didn't make the cut, so to speak, when the various scriptures were assembled into a canon for Jews and Christians respectively.

THE BOOK OF JUBILEES

One such lost book of the Bible is the Book of Jubilees, which contains many interesting details not included in the original books of the Bible, though the Bible was used as source material throughout.

   According to the Microsoft Encarta Encyclopedia (2001), the Book of Jubilees was written about 100 B.C. It is also known under the names "The Lesser Genesis," "The Apocalypse of Moses," and "The Testament of Moses."

   "Modern Biblical scholars," the article states, "generally agree that Jubilees was written by a single unknown author, who probably was a Levite priest or a Pharisee. Hebrew most likely was the language of the original; substantial portions of the book written in Hebrew were discovered in Qumran in 1947."

The reader is probably already aware that Qumran is where the Dead Sea Scrolls were discovered, and the Book of Jubilees was therefore possibly an influence on Christ himself, given the timeframe shortly before Jesus' ministry and the influence exerted by the Essenes on the Jewish culture that followed quickly after them.

"The purpose of the work," the Microsoft Encarta Encyclopedia article continues, "seems to have been to encourage greater devotion to the Torah, or Law, at a time when Judaism was undergoing strong alien influences. The book consists of a history of the world, purportedly revealed by an angel to Moses on Mount Sinai. Much of the historical account, mostly of a legendary nature, is added to the Biblical account in Genesis and Exodus in order to demonstrate the supremacy of the Torah, and all objectionable acts and practices of the Hebrews and the Hebrew patriarchs recounted in the Bible are omitted."

In other words, the author of Jubilees rewrote history, at least as it was recorded up to that time, so that none of the shockingly bad sins of the historical Hebrews would taint the author's attempt to make it appear that the ancient Jews had devotedly followed the laws of Moses—in most cases before those laws had even been set down. For instance, there is no mention of Lot lying with his own daughters in the wake of the destruction of Sodom and Gomorrah. Instead, in order to emphasize the eternal nature of the law, the sins of the various characters are whitewashed so that they appear obedient and faithful in all things.

SATAN PLEADS HIS CASE

One of the most interesting aspects of the Book of Jubilees is the additions to and variations from the standard telling of stories in Genesis. As an example, there is this bit of scripture featuring Satan.

Chapter Ten of Jubilees states that, "the unclean demons began to lead astray the children of the sons of Noah, and to make them err and destroy them." Noah prays to God for intervention, and God orders that all the demons be bound and taken away.

Satan then asks God to leave him one-tenth of the demons to be obedient to Satan, so that he can continue to exercise his will upon the wicked. Surprisingly, God agrees and only nine-tenths of the demons are forced to descend into "the place of condemnation." God also teaches Noah the ways of medicine known to the demons, together with their "seductions," so that the righteous will know how to cope with the remaining demons on earth. "Thus the evil spirits were precluded from hurting the Sons of Noah."

Noah dies at age 950. Meanwhile, Noah's descendants descend into the prophesied state of warfare and widespread evil, and "malignant spirits assisted and seduced them into committing transgression and uncleanness." Satan exerts himself to do all this with the help of the demons who were put in his charge. Apparently, ten percent was still enough to keep Satan in business.

SEXUAL COMPLICATIONS ABOUND

There are many Biblical stories that revolve around sex. One involves Rueben, one of Jacob's sons and a patriarch in his own right, who lies with his father's concubine, Bilhah. When Bilhah awakens and sees Rueben lying beside her, she cries out in her shame. She confesses to Jacob that she is now unclean since she was defiled by Rueben. Jacob is greatly angered by what has happened, and never goes to Bilhah sexually again.

Rueben has broken the Law, having "uncovered his father's skirt," the penalty for which is the death of both the man and the woman involved. "Cursed be he who lies with the wife of his father, for he has uncovered his father's shame." Under the laws of Moses, it is impossible to atone for this sin, but Rueben is allowed to live since the law had not been revealed yet in his time.

The Book of Jubilees also tells the story of Onan, a son of Judah, who is commanded to father children with his late brother's wife. This was in fact part of the Law, intended to give the dead a kind of offspring in their absence. Onan goes into his sister-in-law's home, but "spilled his seed on the ground" in defiance of the commandment. It has been debated whether the spilling of his seed involved masturbation or coitus interruptus, but in either case it was a sin for which God struck Onan dead.

SATAN AGAIN REARS HIS UGLY HEAD

The Book of Jubilees winds down with a quick retelling of the early part of the Exodus story, and includes another interesting variation involving Satan. In the story of the Israelites fleeing Pharaoh, Satan appears and tries to aid the Egyptians in stopping the Israelites from crossing the Red Sea. In fact, there are several references to Satan in Jubilees, who always appears in an effort to stymie the righteous Jews in their historical struggles.

This is particularly noteworthy because in the original telling of these stories in the Old Testament, Satan is not mentioned at all. The Old Testament references to Satan can pretty much be counted on one hand, though he figures more prominently in the New Testament. Given the fact that Jubilees was written about 100 B.C., the emergence of Satan as a visible enemy can be observed to increase as time passes, perhaps indicating a shift in thinking regarding the origin of evil and even a belated admission of the real-world presence of the enemy of all mankind.

But the Book of Jubilees promises the eventual liberation from the devil. "And there shall be no more a Satan, or any evil one, and the land shall be clean from that time forever more."

The return to the former paradise of Eden, the completion of a long and arduous cycle of judgment and redemption, this time without the presence of a tempter to lead the gullible child Man astray, is perhaps the greatest dream that can ever be dreamed. What the author of Jubilees seems to be trying to say is that that dream cannot be achieved without a proper reverence for the Law, a Law that is eternal and unchanging throughout all time. "Think not," Jesus said in the Gospels, "that I have come to change the Law and the prophets. I have not come to change them, but to fulfill them."

In that fulfillment, the Book of Jubilees says, is the true freedom of mankind.

WHERE DID JASHER COME FROM?

The Book of Jasher has a long and controversial history. While some dispute its authenticity, others regard it as a sacred work of scripture worthy of deep and scholarly study. What is offered here is some of the history of the book and a brief overview of many of the more fascinating stories it contains.

A search for the Book of Jasher on the Internet lists a wealth of links to analysis of the mysterious work, including an article written by Mormon scholar John P. Pratt for *Meridian Magazine* in January of 2002. The Mormons take the Book of Jasher very seriously, since it became available in translation in 1840, about the time the Mormon Church was being created in the deserts of Utah by their prophet Joseph Smith, who quoted from Jasher in his writings at the time as a reliable source.

There are a couple of references to Jasher in the Old Testament, which are often used to argue for the book's authenticity. In the story of Joshua and the Israelites causing the sun and moon to stand still as they made war on their enemies, from the Biblical book of Joshua, the author asks rhetorically, "Is this not written in the Book of Jasher?" (Joshua 10:13) Later, in the Book of Second Samuel, King David instructs the Jews in the use of archery, with the author declaring, "Behold, it is written in the Book of Jasher." (2 Samuel 1:18) The point being that Jasher somehow preexisted the more familiar books of the Bible and was regarded as an authentic source by their authors.

"There are at least three books published in modern times," Pratt writes, "which have been called 'The Book of Jasher.' One is a Hebrew treatise on ethics, for which no one makes the claim of being a lost book of scripture. Another is an easily detected fraud, published in 1751, which claims to have been translated into English by Flaccus Albinus Alcuinus. It is still in print, so if you obtain a copy of the Book of Jasher, make sure it is not that one. It is sometimes called Pseudo-Jasher to distinguish it from the third book of Jasher, which is a legitimate Hebrew document."

The name Jasher is sometimes incorrectly assumed to be that of the author, which the fraudulent version of the book claims as well. But the Hebrew word Jasher derives from "straight" and is often translated as "right" or "upright," Platt informs us. It is usually interpreted to mean the book is an accurate and trustworthy account of Jewish history, and that the character of its author is trustworthy.

THE STORY OF JASHER BEGINS

The Book of Jasher opens with the story of creation and continues through until the time of the Book of Judges in the Bible. Throughout its retelling of the Genesis stories, it offers many tantalizing bits of detail not included in the standard Biblical accounts.

For instance, in the narrative of events leading up to the Great Flood, the character of Cainar is introduced, a man so wise that he rules over spirits and demons. He has advance knowledge of the coming deluge, and he bears witness to some of the evils done in the meantime. One of those evils is this: some of the men give their wives a potion to drink that renders them barren in order that the women won't lose their figures and their beauty through bearing children. It is similar to a story told in the apocryphal Book of Enoch, where evil angels teach mankind the science of abortion, of "smiting the child inside the womb."

The death of Cain is told in the early chapters, a death strange and completely accidental. A man called Lamech, who is nearly blind and must be led around by his son, Tubal Cain, is walking with his son in a field when the original Cain, the son of Adam, approaches them. They slay Cain with arrows in the mistaken belief that he is an animal, being too far away to see him clearly. (The Lord has at last requited Cain's evil.) Lamech and Tubal Cain come to see the slain "animal," and realize they have killed Cain. In his grief, Lamech claps his hands, and in doing so accidentally kills his son Tubal. Lamech's wives then seek to kill him as well, but in the end decide to just separate themselves from him. Lamech protests that he is nearly blind, and had slain Cain and Tubal Cain unknowingly. His wives forgive him and return to him, but they bear him no more children because God is growing increasingly angry over the evil done on the earth.

The birth of Enoch follows soon after. As in the Book of Enoch, he is a man whom God allows to see the truth in visions. At one point, Enoch ascends into heaven in a whirlwind, with horses and chariots of fire, the familiar UFO trip to meet God told of in Ezekiel and elsewhere. After the Enoch story, Noah is born, and again the Book of Jasher tells the story a little differently.

In Jasher, the Lord offers mankind a period of 120 years to clean up its act before he destroys them with the flood. Noah decides to father no children in the meantime, but God promises that He will guard Noah's children because of Noah's righteousness. When mankind, predictably, does not repent in the allotted time, Noah is told to begin building the ark. When the time comes for the deluge, the wicked gather around the ark and beg to be let in, but Noah refuses, citing the 120-year grace period. Meanwhile, those safely in the ark are tossed around by the violence of the waves and begin to suffer great anxiety and to fear death. Noah begs God for help and the Lord answers him by stopping the rain. The ark comes to rest upon the mountains of Ararat.

ADDING SATAN TO THE MIX

Fast-forward to the story of Abraham being instructed to sacrifice his son Isaac. This time the narrative begins with Isaac boasting to his half-brother Ishmael that Isaac would make himself a willing sacrifice. God hears Isaac speaking, and is pleased with Isaac's words. Satan appears before God, and they converse. Satan argues that men love God only when he gives them gifts, and then quickly forget about him. Satan contends that now that Abraham has his son Isaac, Abraham has forsaken God.

God counters by saying that Abraham is upright, and would not withhold Isaac if he were asked to give him up. Satan then challenges God to put Abraham to the test. All of this recalls the opening of the Book of Job, in which God and Satan wrangle over Job's righteousness and gratitude before God sends horrifying torments to test Job's faith.

As in the Genesis version, God tells Abraham to sacrifice Isaac, which Abraham agrees to do, a little unwillingly at first. Abraham lies to Sarah, telling her that he is taking Isaac to study with Shem, a son of Noah. Sarah approves of his plan, though she is grieved to be separated from Isaac for even a short period of time. Ishmael and Abraham's servant Eliezer accompany Abraham and Isaac, and Ishmael boasts that after Isaac's death, Ishmael will inherit as Abraham's only son. Eliezer says that he, not Ishmael, will inherit.

As the four men are traveling, Satan appears to Abraham as a very aged man and asks Abraham if he is "silly or brutish" in his willingness to sacrifice Isaac. Satan tells him the order could not possibly be from God. Abraham recognizes Satan in spite of his disguise and rebukes him. Satan leaves. Satan next appears to Isaac as a handsome young man. Satan asks Isaac if he is aware of Abraham's plan to sacrifice him. Isaac asks his father if he has heard Satan's words, and Abraham tells him not to heed Satan.

Abraham again rebukes Satan and Satan leaves. Satan next takes the form of a large brook with mighty waters. The four men nearly drown trying to cross the brook, but Abraham recognizes the area and realizes there is no brook there. Abraham again rebukes Satan, which terrifies the devil and the place returns to its normal state as dry land.

They approach the place of the sacrifice, and see a "pillar of fire" reaching from the earth to heaven, and a cloud of glory with the Lord inside. Readers of UFO literature will again recognize the familiar descriptions of a column of light extending from a ship, called here "a cloud of glory."

Isaac confirms what Abraham sees, but Ishmael and Eliezer see nothing at all and therefore do not accompany Abraham and Isaac any further. A case of certain individual witnesses being "Chosen Ones," as is frequently seen in UFO literature?

When they reach the mountain, Isaac asks Abraham where the sacrificial lamb is, and Abraham informs Isaac that he will be the sacrifice instead. Isaac says he will do as the Lord has spoken "with joy and cheerfulness of heart." Isaac even helps to build the altar on which he will be sacrificed. Isaac then asks that after he has been made a burnt offering that his ashes be taken home to his mother Sarah. Both Abraham and Isaac weep bitterly. Isaac is bound to the altar and Abraham raises the knife. Angels of mercy appear and beg God to spare Isaac. God appears and tells Abraham He has relented because of Abraham's faith.

A ram appears as a substitute sacrifice, and the author says the ram was prepared for that moment since the beginning of time, implying that God never truly intended to have Abraham sacrifice Isaac. There is another variation here having to do with Satan. Satan had caused the ram to be caught in a thicket by his horns so that Abraham would not see it in time to avert the sacrifice of Isaac. Abraham sees Satan attempting to withhold the ram, but lays hands on it anyway and carries out the intended sacrifice.

Satan next appears to Sarah and tells her that Abraham has already sacrificed Isaac. Sarah weeps and mourns. She travels to Hebron and begins to make inquiries about Abraham and Isaac. Again Satan appears to Sarah and admits he has lied about Isaac being sacrificed. Sarah literally dies from happiness on the spot. Meanwhile, Abraham and Isaac return home to find Sarah gone and are told she went to Hebron looking for them. They go to Hebron after her, and learn of Sarah's death. They weep bitterly together once again.

The inclusion of Satan in the familiar sacrifice narrative is an eerie accompaniment to an already eerie story. Were a person in our time to report   hearing a voice that told him to murder his child, he would immediately be put away as criminally insane. It is interesting to see here that Satan is sent to dissuade Abraham from carrying out the act of sacrifice, while in modern times he would more likely be seen as encouraging the act of ritual slaughter.

ARE HOLOGRAMS A WEAPON OF GOD?

The story of Jacob and Esau is retold in Jasher as well, with a very interesting difference offered that may relate to current developments in modern psychological warfare. There is a moment when Esau, the cheated and disgraced elder brother of Jacob, plots to kill Jacob in revenge for so many insults. Jacob learns of Esau's plan and calls upon the Lord for help. God sends three angels to help Jacob. The angels then appear to Esau as two thousand men equipped with weapons of war, and Esau is terrified and flees along with his troops.

The idea has been kicked around for many years now of the possible use of holograms to create false images, as on a battlefield, to terrify the enemy into submission. For instance, as in the case of Jacob's angels above, holograms might be utilized to create the illusion that there are huge armies or weapons technologies that the opposing forces cannot stand against. The use of holograms as religious propaganda has also been reported, as in the case of the mass sightings of the Virgin Mary in Cuba in the early 1980s. Perhaps mankind is beginning to catch up with a form of hologram technology first practiced on the battlefields of the Bible by the advanced beings we call angels?

There is another similar incident a short time later in Jasher in which Jacob and his sons find themselves greatly outnumbered by a foreign enemy. Again, a battlefield hallucination is employed by God to help deliver the Jews militarily.

"For the Lord caused them to hear the voice of chariots and the voice of mighty horses from the sons of Jacob, and the voice of a great army accompanying them. And these kings were seized with great terror at the sons of Jacob."

Now that is some real "psychological warfare," is it not? This further illustrates one of the great themes of both Jasher and the Jews throughout history: in spite of being on the surface a small, nearly defenseless people at times, by the help of their God they have conquered and outlasted innumerable enemies, from the days of Biblical history to our own times. The 19th century British statesman, Benjamin Disraeli, was asked if he knew of any proof of God's existence, and his reply was, "The Jew, sir. The Jew." The survival of the Jewish race and the Jewish faith seem simply miraculous to some, miraculous enough to justify believing in their God as well.

There is yet another possible hologram experience in the Book of Jasher. In the version of the life of Moses told in Jasher, Moses grows to manhood and sees how his people suffer as slaves. Moses asks Pharaoh to grant the Jews a day of rest on the seventh day, and Pharaoh relents and does as he asks. Moses is out walking one day when he sees an Egyptian taskmaster beating one of Moses' Hebrew brethren. Moses kills the Egyptian and buries him in the sand. Moses soon realizes that his crime is known, and Pharaoh orders that Moses be slain. Suddenly an angel appears to Pharaoh. The angel cuts off the head of the captain of Pharaoh's guards, but at the same time creates the illusion that he has killed Moses instead—still another instance of a hologram being superimposed over reality and used as a life-saving deception.

THE BOOKS OF ENOCH

The apocryphal Books of Enoch are a marvelous addendum to the Bible as we more commonly know it. We share in Enoch's wondrous adventure as he travels to both heaven and hell, bearing witness to the innumerable mysteries and testifying always for the sake of the righteous as they battle, suffer and endure the wicked. The fall of the evil angels called The Watchers, who take earthly wives and breed a horrifying race of giants; the birth of Noah as a strange and supernatural child of the great unknown who utterly terrifies his father; the creation story told by God, which begins with God as a solitary figure creating the visible from the invisible, all combine to fascinate and enthrall the reader who takes up the Books of Enoch and joins the prophet on his fearsome ride through the cosmos. Space and time melt away, and the promise of an eventual paradise where there is no time becomes the goal of Enoch's journey, and our own as well.

While much has been written about the first Book of Enoch, it is perhaps more appropriate here to discuss the lesser-known Enoch Two: The Secrets of Enoch.

Enoch is introduced as a wise man much beloved by God who is given to see the wonders of the heavenly realm, including the "inexpressible singing of the host of the cherubim and of the boundless light." Enoch's story begins when he is 165-years-old and begets Methuselah. Enoch then lived another 200 years, for a total of 365. As he lies on his couch asleep, he begins to cry—still in his sleep—completely at a loss to explain his distress.

Two men appear to him, so large there is nothing like them on earth. Their faces, eyes and lips all shine and burn with fire, and they have the telltale wings of angels. They call Enoch by name, and he is roused from his sleep to see that the two "men" are indeed really there. Enoch salutes them and is seized with fear. The angels tell him to have courage. They are sent by God to take him into heaven. Enoch is instructed to tell his sons that he will be gone for a while, and that they are not to look for him until he returns.

The angels bear Enoch on their wings to the first heaven and place him on the clouds. He is shown how angels control the houses of the snow and dew. On to the second heaven, where he is shown rebellious angels being punished as prisoners in a terrible darkness. Enoch pities them, and they ask him to pray to God on their behalf. On to the third heaven. Enoch is shown an idyllic garden with a wondrous fragrant tree. He states that paradise "is between corruptibility and incorruptibility." The garden is guarded over by three hundred angels.

Enoch is told the paradise is prepared for the righteous, who suffer greatly yet do good works in the world. Next, Enoch is shown a place of darkness and torture for the punishment of sinners, who practice sodomy and witchcraft and oppress the poor. The fourth heaven is taken up by an astronomical lesson on the goings of the sun and the moon. In the fifth heaven, Enoch sees a race of giant soldiers, called the Grigori, with withered faces and silent mouths. The angels tell him the Grigoris fell with Satan and impregnated the daughters of men to produce the familiar race of giants who "befouled the earth with their deeds." After being questioned by Enoch, the giant soldiers break into song, asking God to pity them. In the sixth heaven, Enoch sees seven bands of angels who guard the sun and moon and stars and regulate events on earth, including world governments and the natural world of rivers and forests, as well as recording all the deeds of mankind. In the seventh heaven, Enoch sees a "very great light and fiery troops of great archangels." These fearsome soldiers serve God with joyful singing.

After showing Enoch the seventh heaven, the two angels leave him alone, which causes Enoch great fear and he cries out for help. Gabriel comes to him. "Gabriel caught me up, as a leaf caught up by the wind." Enoch sees the eighth and ninth heavens, which include the twelve signs of the Zodiac. Finally, in the tenth heaven, Enoch sees the face of God, "like iron made to glow in fire," and emitting sparks. The Lord's face is "ineffable, marvelous, and very awful, and very, very terrible. And who am I to tell of the Lord's unspeakable being and of his very wonderful face?" The Lord instructs the Angel Michael to dress Enoch in "the garments of glory." Enoch is then taught the ways of heaven and earth and writes 366 books of the knowledge that he is given.

God tells Enoch that He was alone before He made creation. Then He made light from the darkness and the visible from the invisible. There follows a wonderful creation story where God speaks in surprising detail and frankness, a much more direct, "first-person" account than is found in Genesis. It begins with the creation of angels as troops with fiery weapons. The Genesis pattern of seven days of creation is also used here in Enoch's version, with man again being created on the sixth day. But there are fascinating differences, namely the "seven consistencies" from which man was made.

First, his flesh was made from the earth. Second, his blood from the dew. Third, his eyes from the sun. Fourth, his bones from stone. Fifth, his intelligence from the swiftness of the angels and the clouds. Sixth, his veins and his hair from the grass of the earth. And seventh, his soul from the breath of God and from the wind.

As in Genesis, God then rests on the seventh day. But God also talks of an eighth day, a day without time or the measurement of time. "A time of not counting, endless, with neither years nor months nor weeks nor days nor hours."

Enoch is then told to return to earth for thirty days to tell his household what he has seen and to write down his journey for the sake of future generations. Enoch is returned to the couch on which he slept at the book's beginning, where his son Methuselah has been keeping watch for him and is amazed to see his return. Enoch, with weeping, tells of how being in the Lord's presence is "endless pain." Enoch also tells his son he now knows everything, being shown the utter and complete truth of mortal and universal existence by God.

Again, details of the workings of astronomy and the natural world are recited, which are then followed by exhortations to be righteous and to give no unclean gifts to God. Enoch tells his sons that the fate of man's soul is fixed even before he is born. God bids us to be meek, to endure attacks and insults, and not to offend widows and orphans. Enoch instructs his sons to pass along his books to others, then begins to speak of how it is important to treat the poor well. The moral injunctions Enoch speaks of are all familiar from the Old Testament, but there is an urgency and intensity to Enoch's version that stems mostly from the strangeness of his journey and the fact that he will be taken again by the angels, this time for good.

The word of Enoch's impending departure into heaven becomes widely known, and two thousand men arrive to kiss him goodbye and ask his blessing. Enoch again prophesies a world where time is not measured, a paradise that cannot be corrupted, and says those gathered to see him off must walk before the Lord in "terror and trembling."

The Lord sends darkness on the earth. Enoch is taken up, and the light returns. Enoch's sons erect an altar at the place where Enoch has been taken up, and make sacrifices there. The people and the elders gather together for a great feast with his sons, and they make merry for three days, praising God, who had favored them with the sign of Enoch's heavenly departure, the story of which is to be handed down from generation to generation and from age to age.

SOME FINAL THOUGHTS ON ENOCH

The events described in Enoch Two are very similar to what we read in modern-day UFO abduction accounts. The standard scenario in which the abductee finds himself partially awake, but in a dreamlike state, is then taken up from his bed and transported into another world with very different qualities from the normal waking world, accompanied by men or angels or the now familiar gray aliens, can be seen to be linked in Enoch Two with a tradition stretching back thousands of years. The spiritual mysteries of one age are continued in the next, and perhaps we can draw comfort from believing that the Eighth Day that God speaks of in Enoch Two, a day when no time is measured, may be just around the corner on the Cosmic Calendar.

Chapter Nineteen
Gnosticism And The Occult

- Read about the use that world famous occultist Madame H.P. Blavatsky made of the Gnostic scriptures. Did she truly free her mind from orthodox religion?

- Why did the psychoanalyst Carl G. Jung have such a fondness for the Gnostics? Is individual revelation superior to the orthodox collective experience?

- Does a poem written by Jung contain some core truths about the nature of the Gnostic God? Is God really both good and evil simultaneously?

The modern roots of Gnosticism run deeply into the past, even though the Nag Hammadi library was found only in the first half of the last century. But fragments of some of the books have been known for hundreds of years, and their influence has been felt for some time.

A REBELLION AGAINST THE ORTHODOX

One example of Gnostic influence on occult thinking dates back to the 1880s, to the London flat of the world famous occultist Madame H.P. Blavatsky. According to the After-Word of **The Nag Hammadi Library In English**, written by Richard Smith, "It was Madame Blavatsky who first claimed the Gnostics as precursors for the occult movement. In her program to divide speculative learning into esoteric and exoteric, truth and religion, the Gnostics were an obvious opposition to what she called 'Churchianity.' She absorbed the Gnostics, in her universal, free-associative style, into a great occult synthesis."

Smith then quotes Blavatsky's writings thusly: "Ialdabaoth, the creator of the material world, was made to inhabit the planet Saturn according to the Ophites."

Blavatsky thus employs the negative version of the creator God, discussed throughout this book, as a means of freeing the inquisitive mind from the restrictions of orthodox Christianity. If the material world is of itself evil, then rebellion against that world can only be a saintly kind of warfare.

Smith goes on to say that, "There is an esoteric tradition, Blavatsky felt, within every religion teaching her 'secret doctrine.'"

"The Gnosis," Blavatsky herself writes, "or traditional 'secret knowledge,' was never without its representatives in any age or country."

She explained the Catholic Church's persecution of the Gnostics as being because of the church's "intense and cruel desire to crush out the last vestige of the old philosophies, by perverting their meaning, for fear that their own dogmas should not be rightly fathered on them." In other words, to stamp out the competition and keep the much older secret Gnostic doctrines out of the marketplace of ideas because they may disprove much of what Catholics take to be the Gospel truth.

"H.P. Blavatsky and her Theosophical Society wrote the book on secret traditions," Smith says. "Most esoteric movements ever since have found it almost impossible to step outside of her (sometimes unconscious) influence."

With credentials like that to back her up, one cannot easily overestimate the enormous impact that Gnosticism, as filtered through Blavatsky, has had on the current state of occult philosophy.

CARL G. JUNG AND THE GNOSTICS

Another famous name among the occultists is that of the psychiatrist Carl G. Jung. He continually referred to the Gnostics in his writings and loved to be photographed wearing his Gnostic ring. On his birthday in 1952, he was given as a gift a recently discovered Gnostic papyrus manuscript, containing some of the books also found at Nag Hammadi.

Smith says that Jung wrote so often about the Gnostics simply because he liked them. In a book called *Psychological Types*, Jung wrote about "the vastly superior [compared to that of the Church] intellectual content of gnosis, which in the light of our present mental development, has not lost but considerably gained in value." Jung also applauds its "Promethean and creative spirit. We find in Gnosticism what was lacking in the centuries that followed: a belief in the efficacy of individual revelation and individual knowledge. This belief was rooted in the proud feeling of man's affinity with the gods, subject to no human law, and so overmastering that it may even subdue the gods by the sheer power of gnosis."

Which says a great deal about the power of Gnosticism to raise one's self-esteem, given that it puts the believer in a position to "subdue" even his own gods.

THE INDIVIDUAL VERSUS THE COLLECTIVE

But again the most basic understanding of how Gnosticism and the occult complement each other probably lies in the realm of freedom for the individual to experiment and learn and grow from his introspection, to find the divine within himself as an individual as opposed to the collective religious experience, as in a typical orthodox Church. Some Gnostics believe in a God who embodies both good and evil at the same moment.

Jung wrote a poem about that concept in 1916 that includes the lines:

"Abraxas [a Gnostic name for God] begetteth truth and lying, good and evil, light and darkness, in the same word and in the same act.

"Wherefore is Abraxas terrible.

"It is love and love's murder.

"It is the saint and his betrayer.

"It is the brightest light of day and the darkest night of madness."

Steering that course between light and dark, between sunny sanity and nighttime insanity, is a fate experienced by everyone, whether they practice Gnosticism or not. Perhaps the primary question to ask is this: Does individual revelation mean that you're truly going it alone? Or does one in fact eventually make contact with the divine spark that dwells both inside and outside of every living soul? Is knowledge of the self also the knowledge of all mankind and of the God who may yet someday deliver us?

Questions like these can only be answered, again, by the individual, and it is the individual who stands to profit or lose from the kind of deep soul searching that Gnostic belief requires. It isn't easy, as the scriptures discussed in this book bear witness. But when has seeking after the truth ever been an easy process?

About The Author

Sean Casteel received his B.A. in Journalism from the University of Oklahoma in 1985. He has written about UFOs, alien abduction and other paranormal subjects since 1989. He was at one time a contributing editor to "UFO Magazine" and a regular contributor to "Fate Magazine" and "Mysteries Magazine." Casteel's previous books for Inner Light/Global Communications include *UFOs, Prophecy and the End of Time* and *Signs and Symbols of the Second Coming*. He is the coauthor, with Timothy Green Beckley, of *Our Alien Planet: This Eerie Earth*.

Sources and Recommended Reading

The Nag Hammadi Library In English
General Editor James M. Robinson
Harper and Row, 1978 and 1988

The Gnostic Gospels
Elaine Pagels
Vintage Books, 1979

Occidental Mythology: The Masks of God
Joseph Campbell
Penguin Books, 1964

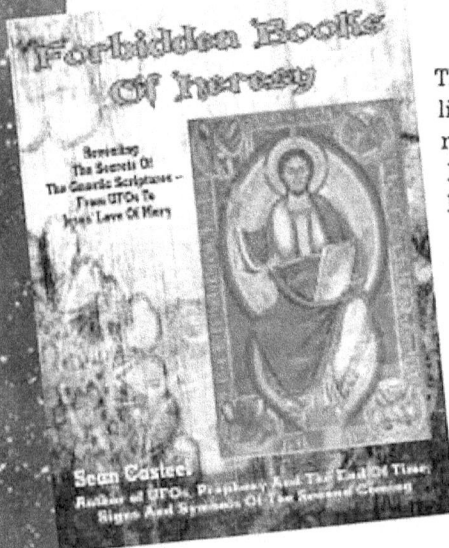

THE ARK OF THE COVENANT, AND OTHER SECRET WEAPONS OF THE ANCIENTS

Here is proof the ancients possessed "secret technology" that made them exceptional warriors. They might even have had the capability to annihilate their formidable foes utilizing nuclear-like devices. The question is how did they come about such an innovative science? Did they develop such devices on their own? Did God give the "chosen" unheralded power over their enemies? Or were ancient astronauts somehow involved? **David Medina**, along with **Sean Casteel, Tim Beckley, Olav Phillips, Brad Steiger** and **Tim R. Swartz** tackle an intriguing subject that gives evidence to the fact that the ancients had supernatural powers that were often lethal. For the first time, here is a detailed analysis of the mysterious *Ark of the Covenant*. Learn how the Ark was built and housed, and how the priests that tended it were required to wear protective clothing to shield them from what we call today nuclear energy. Moses even used the Ark to create a "controlled earthquake" to punish a rebellion by some of the Israelites. The desert ground opened up and swallowed the rebels. Also discover information on astounding air battles, and a very advanced type of "Thunderbolt Energy" that caused catastrophic disasters. There are also the issues of Magical Swords and superior aircraft mentioned in various ancient texts. This work contains fascinating insight into high-tech, death-dealing devices that predate our own by millennia.

8.5x11—Illustrated—ISBN-13: 978-1606111819—$19.95

THE CHARISMATIC, MARTYRED LIFE OF JOAN OF ARC—

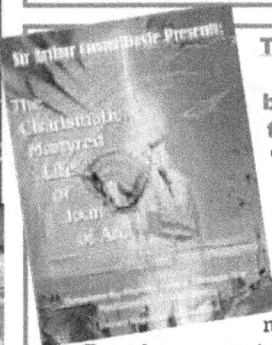

by Sir Arthur Conan Doyle with an introduction by Sean Casteel. **Warning! This is NOT an ordinary historical reference.** Instead this work has been transmitted across time and space through a French medium as translated by the creator of Sherlock Holmes. It may be a book that Joan of Arc helped write herself. For how did mysterious disembodied voices lead a young French peasant girl to military leadership and victories in battle for her beloved France? This was definitely not written by the author — one of the most acclaimed spiritualist mediums of his time — by "ordinary means" — instead, it came directly "from spirit." It is an historical paranormal adventure that provides insight into a remarkable charismatic individual. .

8.5x11—188 pages—ISBN-13: 978-1606110782—$19.95

SIGNS AND SYMBOLS OF THE SECOND COMING (Updated/Expanded Edition)

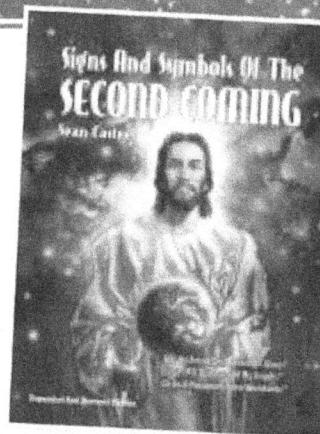

Author Sean Casteel maintains millions worldwide are awaiting the return of the Christ which could take place in our lifetime. Opinions on the Second Coming vary. "For example, there is a general consensus among a large group of UFO believers that we should await some form of open, mass landing of UFOs seen around the world. But, what if this expectation is not fulfilled until the Battle of Armageddon? Perhaps we are mistaken looking for a 'morally indifferent' landing on the White House lawn and should instead anticipate a vengeful mass landing in which the often seen flying saucers return to destroy the armies gathered by the Antichrist and establish the millennial reign of Jesus." The author speculates further as to the possible use of holograms to stage a "false flag" Second Coming and offers a checklist of signs and wonders to watch for in the countdown to the Day of the Lord.

8.5x11—104 pages—ISBN-13 978-1606111741
$14.95

SCANDALS OF THE POPES, AND THE PROPHECIES OF SAINT MALACHI
by Arthur Crockett.

There is more to the history of the Vatican than the public knows about, including the Scandals of Great Popes. Levitation and Teleportation of the Popes. The Mysterious Box No Pope Will Open. St. Malachi's Prophecy of the Popes. The Strange Story of Pope Joan. Pope Benedict XIV: Did He Write A Book On Miracles? The Vatican and Satanism. The Church's Obsession with Aliens. (Add $13 for related DVD)

8.5x11—ISBN-13: 978-1606111826—$14.95

SUPER SPECIAL: All 7 books listed on pages 4 and 5 just $105.00 + $12.00 S/H (U.S. only!)

Timothy Beckley · Box 753
New Brunswick, NJ 08903

Inner Light/Global Communications
P.O. Box 753
New Brunswick, NJ 08903

Email: mrufo8@hotmail.com

www.conspiracyjournal.com

www.ingramcontent.com/pod-product-compliance
Lightning Source LLC
Chambersburg PA
CBHW080534090426
42733CB00015B/2582